DEVIL'S ADVOCATES

DEVIL'S ADVOCATES is a series of books devoted to exploring the classics of horror cinema. Contributors to the series come from the fields of teaching, academia, journalism and fiction, but all have one thing in common: a passion for the horror film and a desire to share it with the widest possible audience.

'The admirable Devil's Advocates series is not only essential – and fun – reading for the serious horror fan but should be set texts on any genre course.'
Dr Ian Hunter, Reader in Film Studies, De Montfort University, Leicester

'Auteur Publishing's new Devil's Advocates critiques on individual titles... offer bracingly fresh perspectives from passionate writers. The series will perfectly complement the BFI archive volumes.' **Christopher Fowler,** *Independent on Sunday*

'Devil's Advocates has proven itself more than capable of producing impassioned, intelligent analyses of genre cinema... quickly becoming the go-to guys for intelligent, easily digestible film criticism.' *Horror Talk.com*

'Auteur Publishing continue the good work of giving serious critical attention to significant horror films.' *Black Static*

 DevilsAdvocatesbooks

DevilsAdBooks

DEVIL'S ADVOCATES

THE COMPANY OF WOLVES

JAMES GRACEY

Acknowledgments

Thanks to John Atkinson of Auteur for kindly allowing me the opportunity to write about one of my favourite films, and for his steadfast patience when I strayed from the path. For various reasons, I'd also like to thank Naila Scargill, Shauneen Magorrian, Kate Roddy, Tim Burden, Amber Wilkinson and Christine Makepeace.

Full-mooned howls of eternal thanks and indebtedness to the following for all their support, suggestions and brutal honesty: Alexandra Heller-Nicholas, Jon Towlson, Caroline Ryder, John McAliskey, Emma Kelly and Alastair Crawford. What big eyes you all have.

I would especially like to extend my thanks and sincere gratitude to Tsa Palmer, Suzy McKee Charnas, Hannah Priest and Ernest Mathijs for all their time, kindness, generosity and invaluable insight.

Lastly, thanks to my parents for all their support and encouragement.

First published in 2017 by
Auteur, 24 Hartwell Crescent, Leighton Buzzard LU7 1NP
www.auteur.co.uk
Copyright © Auteur 2017

Series design: Nikki Hamlett at Cassels Design
Set by Cassels Design www.casselsdesign.co.uk

British Library Cataloguing-in-Publication Data
A catalogue record for this book is available from the British Library

ISBN paperback: 978-1-911325-31-4
ISBN ebook: 978-1-911325-32-1

CONTENTS

INTRODUCTION

The Company of Wolves is a dark fantasy film quite unlike any other. A meditation on the horrors of the adult world, and of adult sexuality, as glimpsed through the dreams of an adolescent girl, it amalgamates aspects of horror, the Female Gothic, fairy tales, werewolf films and coming of age parables. Drenched in atmosphere and an eerily sensual malaise, it boasts striking imagery immersed in fairy tale motifs and startling Freudian symbolism. *The Company of Wolves* was Irish film-maker Neil Jordan's second film and his first foray into the realms of Gothic horror. Jordan co-wrote the screenplay with British novelist Angela Carter. It is based upon several short stories from Carter's *The Bloody Chamber* (1979), a collection of reinterpreted classic literary fairy tales told from a piercing feminist perspective. The film incorporates elements from three stories – each a provocative reworking of Little Red Riding Hood (see **Red Hoods, Dark Woods**). The first story is 'The Werewolf', which tells of how Red Riding Hood discovers her ailing Grandmother is actually a werewolf and features a significant motif of werewolf literature and cinema – a severed wolf paw transforming into a human hand. The second story, 'The Company of Wolves', begins as a series of folkloric anecdotes relating to werewolves, and ends with Red Riding Hood seducing a lycanthropic huntsman. It informed the bulk of the screenplay. Lastly, 'Wolf-Alice' tells of a young girl raised by wolves outside the confines of civilised society, eventually coming of age in the lonely castle of a werewolf duke. Aspects of this tale are evident in certain moments of *The Company of Wolves*, particularly in the story Rosaleen tells the wounded wolf.

The Company of Wolves was released in the early eighties, a time when British cinema was largely concerned with conveying kitchen-sink realism and 'favoured small-screen productions, naturalism, and literary texts'.[1] While film-makers such as Mike Leigh and Ken Loach were offering gritty social commentary on Thatcher's downtrodden Britain, Jordan's film invited audiences into a darkly fantastical world populated by werewolves, witches and maidens breaking free from restrictive social shackles. Unravelling as a feverish exploration of a young girl's burgeoning sexuality, the film's unusual narrative structure begins as the girl, Rosaleen (Sarah Patterson), falls asleep and begins to dream. In her dreams she is told stories and within those stories, other stories are being told. These stories and dreams draw the audience deeper and deeper into the dark woods of Rosaleen's psyche, as she finds herself on the cusp of adulthood and further away from any sense of reality. The cautionary stories Rosaleen's Granny (Angela Lansbury) tells her – of men who are 'hairy on the inside' and of ravening beasts lurking in the forest waiting for young girls to stray from the path – are intended to instil within Rosaleen a fear of being devoured by wolves, and indeed of being devoured sexually, but instead they only arouse her already vivid imagination. Jordan claimed *The Company of Wolves* concerned the coming of age of a young girl who overcomes imagined fears given to her by her grandmother and by implication, society; she gradually realises that these cautionary tales are actually hiding something liberating. The film uses the figure of the werewolf as a metaphor for adult sexuality, a seductive monster imbued with melancholic sensuality. Indeed, the presentation of the werewolf as tragic lover in *The Company of Wolves* is a prelude to the lovelorn vampires in Jordan's later adaptation of Anne Rice's *Interview with the Vampire* (1994). Interestingly, in Rice's *The Tale of the Body Thief* (1992), the fourth novel in her Vampire Chronicles series, *The Company of Wolves* is actually revealed to be one of Lestat de Lioncourt's favourite films.

Rosaleen's curiosity regarding her maturing sexuality is further emphasised throughout the film by recurrent motifs and symbolism – such as phallic snakes draped around outstretched tree branches – that speak of sexual temptation, seduction and loss of innocence. In presenting the coming of age of its young protagonist and her eventual embracement of her sexual desires, *The Company of Wolves* is concerned with the idea of transformation, 'in-between-ness' and 'the related issue of mutability and non-fixity of borders and identities'.[2] Throughout the film these notions are not only explored through the figure of the werewolf as it transforms from human to beast, but through the narrative itself, which takes place within a dream and foregrounds the cultural significance of storytelling (see **Telling Tales**). It posits the girl in a twilight realm that hovers between the waking world and the world of dreams, the world of childhood and the world of adulthood. This is strongly suggested in the opening scenes, which depict the sleeping Rosaleen's bedroom; a room where trinkets and toys of childhood sit alongside adult accoutrements such as the white gown hanging on her door and the make-up on her face. Like the handsome Huntsman who belongs to neither the world of humans nor of wolves, Rosaleen exists in a 'somewhere in-between place'; a transitional space between childhood and adulthood, a space of innocence and curiosity which leads to desire and eroticism.

The Company of Wolves came in the wake of *The Howling* (1981) and *An American Werewolf in London* (1981), two titles which reinvigorated werewolf cinema with stunning special effects and sly humour. As discussed in **The Big Bad Wolf,** the figure of the werewolf has been used throughout literature and cinema to explore the conflict between human intellect and primal instinct; the bestial transformation stripping away civility and notions of order, re-establishing a connection with dormant instincts suppressed through centuries of civilisation. *The Company of Wolves* sets itself apart from most other werewolf films with its literary roots, feminist concerns, art-house execution and by telling its story from the perspective of an adolescent girl. Entwining metaphor with striking visuals and grisly effects, Jordan and Carter's screenplay unblushingly links transformation and lycanthropy with the onset of menstruation as Rosaleen's dreams become increasingly strange and erotic and she begins to embrace her sexuality. These ideas foreshadow those explored in the likes of *Ginger Snaps* (2000) (see **A She-Wolf Came...**), *Teeth* (2007), *Jennifer's Body* (2009) and *It Follows* (2015), all of which depict the horrors of adolescence from the perspective of young women. Throughout her career Carter's writing was informed by feminist principles. In *The Bloody Chamber* she utilised the figures of Red Riding Hood and the werewolf to explore notions of unleashed sexuality and the empowerment of women (see **Seeing Red**). Throughout their screenplay, Jordan and Carter address the traditional roles women play in society, the uneven balance of power, their sexuality, identity and coming of age; *The Company of Wolves* fully acknowledges that women can have the desire to be beastly and are 'equally capable of being transformed into wolves'.[3] Rosaleen's mother affirms this beastly side of women when she tells the girl, 'Whatever beast lurks within men, has its match in women, too.'

Like the dense forest within the dreams of the sleeping girl, Jordan's film bewitches and beguiles as it unfurls in an internalised Gothic mindscape brimming with sensuality and terror; 'a place of all forms of excessive, irrational, and passionate behaviour [...] in which the absence or loss of reason, sobriety, decency and morality is displayed in full horror'.[4]

SYNOPSIS

Present Day. Upon returning home to their large country house from a shopping excursion, a middle-class couple (David Warner and Tusse Silberg) ask their daughter Alice (Georgia Slowe) to fetch her younger sister, Rosaleen (Sarah Patterson), who has taken to her bed with tummy ache. Unable to rouse her drowsing sibling, Alice taunts and mocks her. As Rosaleen falls into a restless sleep she dreams her sister is lost in a dark, foreboding forest, pursued and devoured by a pack of gleaming-eyed, ravenous wolves. Falling deeper into uneasy slumber Rosaleen dreams she lives with her mother and father in a tiny rustic village surrounded by a vast, Grimm fairy tale forest in what appears to be the early nineteenth century. After Alice's funeral Rosaleen is sent to stay with her Granny (Angela Lansbury). As they walk through the forest to Granny's cottage the old woman warns the girl never to stray from the path and to never trust a man whose eyebrows meet in the middle. That night, as Granny begins to knit Rosaleen a bright red shawl, she declares that the worst wolves are 'hairy on the inside' and tells the girl a story about a groom (Stephen Rea) who disappeared on his wedding night after going outside to answer a 'call of nature'. His bride (Kathryn Pogson) searches in vain for him, but, believed eaten by wolves, he is never seen again. The bride remarries and has children, but many years later her first husband returns and, angered by his wife's new family, transforms into a werewolf only to be slain by the woman's new husband who then strikes her as she weeps for the dead groom.

When Rosaleen returns to her mother and father the next day she finds herself the recipient of the romantic advances of an amorous village boy (Shane Johnstone). Awakening in the night, the girl glimpses her parents having sex. Sometime later Granny and Rosaleen visit Alice's grave and Granny presents Rosaleen with the red shawl she's finished knitting and continues to warn the girl about men whose eyebrows meet in the middle. She tells the girl a creepy story about a young man (Vincent McClaren) who meets the Devil (Terence Stamp) in the woods. The Devil, who appears in a Rolls-Royce chauffeured by a young woman with blonde hair (Sarah Patterson), gives the boy an ointment that causes hair to sprout all over his body. As the car drives slowly away, vines wrap themselves around his legs and he screams in horror.

After she attends church with her parents and Granny, Rosaleen goes for a walk through the forest with the amorous boy. When he attempts to kiss her she teases him and runs off to hide, climbing a tall tree and investigating the contents of a stork's nest she discovers in the highest branches. While searching for Rosaleen the amorous boy stumbles upon mutilated animal carcasses and runs to the village to warn that a wolf is lurking in the woods. When Rosaleen arrives home, panic has seized the village. A group of men set out to trap and kill the wolf they believe slaughtered their cattle. Waiting for her father to return, Rosaleen suggests that the wolf might not be what it seems; not worse, just *different*. She tells her mother a story about a young woman (Dawn Archibald) 'done a terrible wrong' by a rich nobleman. Heavily pregnant, she confronts the nobleman at his wedding to another woman and, concluding that the beasts of the forest have more decency than he and his ilk, transforms him and the entire wedding party into wolves. When she gives birth, the woman commands the wolves to serenade her and her baby every night with mournful lupine lullabies.

When he returns home from hunting the wolf, Rosaleen's father discovers to his horror that the forepaw he severed from the carcass has transformed into a human hand. The next day Rosaleen decides to visit her Granny and at her mother's insistence takes a knife to protect herself, though she fearlessly claims she will be safe now the wolf is dead. As she makes her way carefully through the forest Rosaleen encounters a handsome Huntsman (Micha Bergese) who tells her he has been separated from his hunting party. After they share a picnic and it begins to snow, he challenges her to a race to her Granny's, promising to give her what her heart most desires if she wins, and if he wins, she must give him a kiss. Rosaleen continues along the path while the huntsman disappears into the ever-darkening woods. When he arrives at Granny's house he finds the old woman in her rocking chair. Noting that this stranger's eyebrows meet in the middle, Granny strikes him with a red-hot poker from the fire and commands him to return to Hell. Howling in pain the huntsman seizes the poker from Granny and knocks her head clean off with it. Granny's head shatters like porcelain when it collides with the wall. When Rosaleen arrives, she finds the huntsman in her Granny's chair and notices strands of grey hair burning in the fire. When she confronts the huntsman about what he has done with the old woman, he snatches her knife away and suggests she burn her red shawl because she won't need it anymore. As he removes his shirt and Rosaleen remarks on the size of his arms, he replies, 'all the better to hug you with' and reminds her of their bet. When they kiss Rosaleen recoils exclaiming, 'Jesus, what big teeth you have.' He replies, 'All the better to eat you with', prompting the resourceful girl to seize his rifle and shoot him. She watches with a mixture of horror and awe as he transforms into a trembling, whimpering wolf. Taking pity on him Rosaleen whispers, 'I never knew a wolf could cry.'

She comforts the wounded wolf and while soothing him before the fire, tells him a story of a gentle she-wolf who emerges from an underworld through the well in the village. When she is shot by a wary villager the she-wolf seeks refuge in a graveyard and transforms into a young woman (Danielle Dax). An old priest (Graham Crowden) discovers her hiding amongst the headstones and, taking pity on her, consoles her and tenderly dresses her wounds while she quietly weeps. Afterwards, she cautiously returns to her world beneath the village well. Rosaleen concludes, 'She was just a girl after all, who'd strayed from the path in the forest and remembered what she'd found there.'

The next morning Rosaleen's parents, the amorous boy and several of their neighbours from the village search the forest for Rosaleen. Arriving at Granny's cottage, they're startled by a wolf that leaps through the window and dashes into the forest. Cautiously entering the cottage, they see another wolf sitting by the fireplace. Just as Rosaleen's father raises his rifle to shoot the wolf, her mother notices it has Rosaleen's crucifix around its neck and realises the wolf is Rosaleen. She shoves her husband just as he fires and watches as the wolf bounds from the house and into the woods, where she joins her mate. They are soon joined by other wolves as they run through the forest, into the house of the dreaming girl, up the stairs, along the corridor, where they burst into her bedroom. The girl awakens, screaming, as a large wolf crashes through her window.

FOOTNOTES

1. Rockett & Rockett (2003) p38
2. Rockett & Rockett (2003) p37
3. Zipes (2000) p235
4. Botting (2014) p76

CHAPTER ONE: ONCE UPON A TIME

NEIL JORDAN

Neil Jordan was born in Rosses Point, County Sligo, on 25 February, 1950. Prior to embarking on his career as a writer he studied English and History at University College Dublin, graduating in 1971. After collaborating on various theatre and music projects with the likes of Jim and Peter Sheridan, and writing for radio and television, Jordan founded The Irish Writers' Cooperative with Desmond Hogan in 1974 and published his first book, a collection of short stories titled *Night in Tunisia* (1976). The stories and the style in which they were written would feature many themes and ideas that Jordan would revisit throughout his career, including sexual relationships and notions of identity, and an experimental approach to perspective and narrative. *Night in Tunisia* won The Guardian Fiction Prize and was followed by his debut novel, *The Past* (1979), and his first feature film script, *Traveller* (directed by Joe Comerford in 1981). Since then Jordan has published a further five novels: *The Dream of a Beast* (1983), *Sunrise with Sea Monster* (1994), *Shade* (2005), the Gothic-tinged *Mistaken* (2011) and *The Drowned Detective* (2016).

Director John Boorman had admired *Night in Tunisia*, particularly the strong imagery evoked through Jordan's writing, and invited him to collaborate on the screenplay for a film to be called *Broken Dream*. While *Broken Dream* was never filmed, Boorman and Jordan would later collaborate on *Excalibur* (1979). Jordan was credited as Creative Associate and he also directed the documentary *The Making of Excalibur: Myth into Film* (1981), which gave him his first taste of film directing. This experience, along with a strong desire to find new ways to tell stories and a belief that 'Irish writing had gone over the same territory again and again',[1] led him to the world of filmmaking. Set against a backdrop of The Troubles in Northern Ireland, Jordan's feature directorial debut, *Angel* (1982), tells of a show band saxophonist (Stephen Rea) who seeks revenge for the brutal murder of his manager and a mute girl at a dancehall in South Armagh. *Angel* marked Jordan's first collaboration with actor Stephen Rea, who would reappear throughout many of the director's films. While initially intended as a television movie, Channel 4 was so impressed with *Angel* they distributed it theatrically. Critical accolades ensued, including The London Evening Standard's Most Promising Newcomer Award.

While the Northern Irish Troubles frequently form the backdrop of his work, Jordan's unique approach to storytelling helped usher in a new kind of filmmaking in Ireland and radically changed perceptions of Irish culture for international audiences. With each successive film, Jordan's idiosyncratic approach to storytelling became more striking. With the odd exception, Jordan almost always writes his own scripts and his film work ranges from low-key, personal art-house titles such as *Angel, The Miracle* (1991), *The Crying Game* (1992) and *Ondine* (2009), acclaimed and controversial literary adaptations including *The Butcher Boy* (1997), *The End of the Affair* (1999) and *Breakfast on Pluto* (2005), to A-list starring Hollywood films such as *Interview with the Vampire* and *The Brave One* (2007). He frequently surprises with his varied range of themes and interests and a fearless experimentation with form, stylistic approach and subversion of genre conventions. His work, varied as it is, usually features recurring themes such as identity, unconventional sexual relationships and gender roles, the significance of storytelling and the relationship between reality and fantasy, loss of innocence, folk and fairy tales and notions of perception. According to author Carole Zucker, Jordan is 'a postmodern romantic; postmodern in that he destabilises boundaries, appropriates a variety of artistic referents and transfuses genres, romantic in his embrace of perception, intuition and sensation'.[2] He uses imagery and language to convey meaning and is renowned for 'creating moods and situations which can be sensed, but which are too complex to be grasped immediately'.[3] *The Company of Wolves* was Jordan's second film and his first foray into the realms of Gothic horror, a place he would frequently return to throughout his career, both explicitly, as in *Interview with the Vampire, In Dreams* (1999) and *Byzantium* (2012), and in more offbeat ways, as in *High Spirits* (1988) and *The Butcher Boy*. It exhibits many of the director's recurring themes: sexual awakening and identity, the relationship between reality and fantasy, dreams and storytelling, culturally constructed gender relations, and the nature of perception and transformation.

ANGELA CARTER

Angela Carter was born in Eastbourne, on 7 May, 1940. Raised in South Yorkshire, she worked as a journalist for the Croydon Advertiser before studying English and Medieval Literature at Bristol University in 1962. Her first novel, *Shadow Dance*, was published in

1965 and eight others followed: *The Magic Toyshop* (1967), *Several Perceptions* (1968), *Heroes and Villains* (1969), *Love* (1971), *The Infernal Desire Machines of Doctor Hoffman* (1972), *The Passion of New Eve* (1977), *Nights at the Circus* (1984) and *Wise Children* (1991). From 1976 to 1978 she was a fellow in Creative Writing at Sheffield University and from 1980 to 1981 she was visiting professor in the Writing Program at Brown University. While garnering a reputation as a boldly feminist critic and novelist, Carter taught and travelled extensively, living and working in Japan, the United States and Australia, though she always remained 'rooted in a south London sensibility fortified by her grandmother's Yorkshire spirit'.[4]

Throughout her work, Carter explored various recurring themes such as female sexuality, gender roles, fairy tales and storytelling, metamorphosis – both literal and figurative – sexual violence and the deconstruction of patriarchal discourse. Her writing was experimental in style as she drew upon a wide variety of influences, from medieval and Gothic narrative traditions, to science-fiction and horror cinema. Speaking of her love for cinema she once remarked to her friend Sir Christopher Frayling, 'I'm up for anything that flickers'.[5] She greatly admired Hammer horror films and even felt compelled to write to Aida Young, the producer of three of Hammer's *Dracula* films, to explore the idea of working on a screenplay together.

Throughout her career, she also worked as a journalist, contributing to various newspapers and magazines. In addition, she published three works of non-fiction – including *The Sadeian Woman* (1978), a controversial volume of essays exploring the relationship between feminism and pornography – the stage play *Lulu* (1988), various radio plays, two screenplays and several collections of short stories including *Fireworks* (1984), *Saints and Strangers* (1985) and *The Bloody Chamber* – a groundbreaking collection of classic fairly tales retold from a distinctly feminist perspective. Darkly sensual, shockingly violent, erotically charged and populated by frequently ferocious heroines, *The Bloody Chamber* is quite typical of Carter's concerns with psychosexual politics, explorations of the multifaceted nature of women's sexuality and ideas regarding transformation. Carter was unhappy with the way that conventional fairy tales warned young women against acknowledging and exploring their own sexuality. She wanted to retell fairy tales in a way that would make them relevant to modern women and to write about female characters that were empowered by their own sexuality. Carter said her intention was not to do "versions" [of the fairy tales] or, as the American edition of [*The Bloody Chamber*] said, horribly, "adult" fairy tales, but to extract the latent content from the traditional stories'.[6] Amongst the fairy tales Carter reinterpreted are Snow White, Sleeping Beauty, Bluebeard, Beauty and the Beast, Puss-in-Boots and, of course, the tale of Red Riding Hood. Throughout the stories Carter explores ideas concerning female lust; a 'healthy, but also challenging and sometimes disturbing, unbridled and feral lust that delivers up contradictions'.[7]

To investigate the empowerment experienced by women who embrace their sexuality, Carter accentuates the latent sexual undercurrents of the original tales and imbues her heroines with a healthy curiosity regarding their bodies and sexual desires; curiosity that eventually leads to celebratory transformations of a figurative and frequently literal nature. At the heart of her tales is a consideration of the bestial nature of sexuality and the inevitable loss of innocence as characters make the transition from childhood to adulthood. Carter maintained this loss of innocence and corruption of childhood 'isn't necessarily evil, and a person's ability to form a healthy and meaningful adult identity depends on being able to embrace the sexual side of his or her personality, the animal within'.[8]

Interested in the social and cultural construction of gender, Carter not only considered herself a feminist, strongly arguing for a rejection of the identification of women as innocent victims, but also a socialist. She considered fairy tales, folk tales and stories from the oral tradition to be 'the most vital connection we have with the imaginations of ordinary men and women whose labour created our world'.[9] By reinterpreting these tales through a feminist perspective, Carter exposes their misogynistic tone and 'exposes the dangerous appeal of their suggestiveness; she simultaneously retraces and gives substance to the courage and multiple desires of her heroines, who struggle in specific cultural and historical contexts'.[10]

Sadly, Carter died of lung cancer in 1992 at the age of 51 and, according to The Independent, her death 'robbed the English literary scene of one of its most vivacious and compelling voices'.[11]

FROM PAGE TO SCREEN

Jordan and Carter first met in 1979 when he received the Guardian Prize for *Night in Tunisia* and she was a member of the jury panel. The two met again in Dublin in 1982 – several years after the publication of *The Bloody Chamber* and just after Jordan had completed *Angel*. The Irish government had invited writers from all over the world to the city to celebrate the centenary of the birth of James Joyce and Jordan recalls his chance meeting with Carter: 'Jorge Luis Borges read a speech to a thousand or so of Dublin's finest in a plush hotel. No one seemed to know who he was. Halfway through, a *Ceilidh* band struck up next door, drowning him out completely. No one seemed to notice. I asked the head of the Irish Tourist Board to get the band off, and found myself thrown out on the street. Angela had wandered through this baroque extravaganza in a state of bemused wonder. I remember a night's drinking with an Irish lecturer in mediaeval philosophy and a gay priest, the conversation of which consisted mainly of a discourse on farting and the problems of erections on buses. And Angela proved herself to be a model of tact in the face of these, and other, manifestations of the national temperament.'[12] It was during this time the pair talked about adapting her stories for cinema. Carter had previously adapted her story 'The Company of Wolves' for BBC Radio 4 (1980) and had been commissioned by Walter Donohue of Channel 4 to adapt it as a short film.

A week later Jordan received her film script, which was largely based on her radio adaptation, and he admired the darkly sexual motifs Carter coaxed from the stories. Recalling her ability to conjure powerful imagery – something he believed would translate well from page to screen – he claimed 'the single most important factor that drew me to Angela's work – which to me is like nothing else – is that it's both so dramatic and so graphic […] She also has this incredibly fertile imagination and thinks very strongly in terms of imagery'.[13] Jordan believed it was this precise amalgamation of sensuality, savagery and sadism that elevated the core idea far above previous fairy tale adaptations by the likes of Disney, which he considered to be too saccharine. The director noted that what Carter had done was undo 'the way the Victorians, and even the Brothers Grimm, tamed the brutalities and washed out the sensuality of their sources'.[14]

Jordan showed Carter's script to Stephen Woolley, a producer he met at Cannes in 1982. Woolley had previously managed the Scala Cinema near King's Cross in London. A self-confessed admirer of horror and fantasy cinema, he regularly screened classic titles such as Jean Cocteau's *La belle et la bête* (1946), FW Murnau's *Nosferatu* (1922) and Carl Dreyer's *Vampyr* (1932) alongside contemporary titles like Wes Craven's *The Hills Have Eyes* (1977) and John Landis's *An American Werewolf in London*. In the early eighties, Woolley and Nik Powell established Palace Pictures as a specialist video distribution company to promote independently produced British films. As well as distributing the work of film-makers such as Mike Leigh and Peter Greenaway, Palace Pictures gradually began to distribute titles by the likes of John Cassavetes, the Coen brothers, John Waters, Abel Ferrera, Richard Stanley and Sam Raimi. Eventually moving into film production, *The Company of Wolves* was Palace Pictures' first feature film. Given the niche nature of films previously distributed by the company, it's easy to see why Woolley was drawn to Carter and Jordan's project, with its edgy playfulness, art-house sensibilities and refusal to be easily categorised. Werewolf films were also proving popular at this time; *An American Werewolf in London* and *The Howling*, with their state of the art special effects, were able to depict painfully realistic lycanthropic transformations the likes of which had never been seen onscreen before. When he read Carter's initial treatment, Woolley put together a development deal which allowed her and Jordan to flesh out their ideas and write a feature length script.

Jordan went to London and over large quantities of tea at Carter's home in Clapham, the pair planned the script, writing separately and meeting to compare notes. Jordan described Carter's sense of order as exhibiting 'a certain Scots puritan rigor which belies the wicked nature of her work'.[15] The screenplay evolved from the radio adaptation and incorporated elements from all three reinterpretations of Red Riding Hood from *The Bloody Chamber*. The first draft took two weeks to write but Jordan believed it was still too short for a feature film. He suggested they devise a narrative structure in which someone has a dream, and within the dream they are told a story, and within that story other stories are being told, creating a 'Chinese puzzle-box' effect. Jordan drew inspiration from the similarly complex 'Russian Doll' narrative structure of Wojciech Has's *The Saragossa Manuscript* (1964), which he and Carter had both admired. Once they decided to structure the film this way, Jordan remembers the writing flowed 'quite naturally [...] since it gave free rein to Angela's own taste for narrative subversions'.[16]

With the story now structured around an adolescent girl's dream, they agreed that a more surrealistic approach was appropriate. By using the dreams of Rosaleen and the thread of Granny's storytelling within the dreams, they could interweave other stories built around similar themes and lead the audience further away from reality and deeper into a dream-world, where illogical, unexpected things would be glimpsed. Jordan wanted the story to have a realistic beginning, but gradually move into a dream-like, surrealistic space and some of the strangest imagery throughout the film, such as the little porcelain cherubs emerging from the eggs in the stork's nest, was drawn from his own novel, *Dream of a Beast: The sheaves of egg fell away and a cherub stood there, creaking its downy wings. One by one the other eggs split and the cherubs beat their way to the ceiling.*[17]

Jordan's novel unfolds within an increasingly hallucinatory dreamscape as it explores the metaphysical transformation of its narrator, instigated by a sexual relationship he enters with a colleague. The suburbs and cityscapes in which the story takes place gradually become overgrown with strange plants and foliage, as nature progressively encroaches upon civilisation to claim back what has been tamed. The imagery in the final moments of *The Company of Wolves*, as the wolves race through Rosaleen's dilapidated, overgrown home, echoes similar imagery in Jordan's novel.

Jordan and Carter examined every sentence within her stories in order to flesh out the screenplay and create an atmosphere of sensuality and eeriness. One of the most memorable moments of the film comes when a witch (Dawn Archibald) gatecrashes a wedding party and turns the guests into wolves as revenge for the groom's betrayal. In Carter's original story, this moment, based on an ancient Eastern European folk tale, consisted of only two lines: *A witch from up the valley once turned an entire wedding party into wolves because the groom had settled on another girl. She used to order them to visit her, at night, from spite, and they would sit and howl around her cottage for her, serenading her with their misery.*[18] According to Jordan it was fascinating how several lines like this could become a whole segment in the film. He recalled imagining what the valley looked like, how the guests at the wedding party were behaving, contemplating back stories for the groom, the mysterious woman he wronged and 'the pale, haemophiliac visage of the bride he chose'.[19] Carter and Jordan let such images and types of stories come to them in an associative manner and both were adamant that the culmination of the film should be the same as that of the short story: the tale of Red Riding Hood. When it came to the crucial moment in the film when Rosaleen chooses to act upon her feelings for the Huntsman, and her growing acceptance of her own place in the world becomes more obvious, Carter and Jordan felt it was necessary for the character to tell a story of her own that would help to convey her feelings. Jordan devised a variation of Carter's short story 'Wolf-Alice', in which a young girl raised by wolves resists the restrictive conventions of society, all the while slowly realising that she belongs to neither the world of beasts nor the world of man. In Rosaleen's story the wolf turns into a girl – a fairy tale version of Rosaleen – and when she eventually returns to the world below, Jordan suggests this marks a return to her dreaming-self's unconsciousness.

For Jordan, who came to filmmaking from a background of short stories and novels, the writing process was usually an isolated one, but he described working with Carter as an exhilarating experience. Woolley, however, had a less exhilarating experience trying to obtain funding for the project as Channel 4 were apparently unconvinced by the screenplay.[20] They regarded Neil as a 'gentle Irish poet' who had made a rather whimsical IRA thriller and viewed Angela Carter as too intellectual. Woolley claimed they regarded *The Company of Wolves* as a 'vulgar, rather bloody and not particularly appealing thing'[21] and Jordan likened other potential financers to wolves: unpredictable creatures from whom it was difficult to get a rational response. He recalls meeting after meeting in which concern from potential financers was expressed because of the unclassifiable nature of the film. Was it horror? Was it art? What genre did it belong to? Jordan stood by the project though, saying, 'We were blessed with luck, for we had a script that had an inbuilt resistance to any kind of comment. It was a deeply irrational piece of work, outlandish in the way the story moved and simple to the point of naivety in its characters. Quite mad, perhaps, in the end.'[22] Eventually ITC approached Woolley and offered to finance the film, offering £2 million, which Woolley described as quite a 'high' low budget.

A FAIRY TALE DREAM WORLD

The Company of Wolves was always intended to be filmed within the confines of a studio set. It boasts a haunting, otherworldly atmosphere pregnant with wonder and menace. Jordan wanted to create something completely different from his first film, which he thought of as quite realistic in terms of the landscape in which it played out. As *The Company of Wolves* takes place within the dreams of a young girl, he felt this would give him the opportunity to create a world that had never been seen before. Due to complex logistics and lighting, and the need for an environment that could be easily controlled, filming in an actual forest would have been extremely difficult. Before production began though, Jordan did look at several forests in Lyme Regis so as to not limit his options. Despite the restrictive budget, Jordan and Woolley wanted to create something truly cinematic, and during pre-production Jordan worked with Nichola Bruce, a visual artist whose work is primarily concerned with exploring and expressing the mind's ability to composite vision through memory, and Michael Coulson, a graphic artist and film-maker, to create detailed storyboards for the film.

Crucial to the process of creating a never-before-seen sylvan world was production designer and art director Anton Furst. Furst helped design 'Light Fantastic', a ground-breaking holographic art exhibition in London in the late seventies, and worked on Ridley Scott's *Alien* (1979). Furst based his designs on paintings of forests by Gustave Doré and the unusual stylistic qualities of German Expressionist cinema. When discussing the look of the forest both he and Jordan were adamant it should resemble an immense, multi-limbed entity, possess a sinister sensuality, brooding atmosphere and the power to provoke child-like wonder from the audience. To create a forest that would arouse associations with the fairy tales of childhood, Furst also looked to artists such as Pieter Bruegel, John Constable, Salvador Dalí, Richard Dadd, Giovanni Battista Piranesi and, perhaps most significantly, Samuel Palmer. Palmer, a pupil of William Blake and a key figure in Romanticism, specialised in pastoral landscapes. According to Jordan, 'there was a quiet madness to his landscapes, the trees swollen erotically, a church spire listing slightly to one side, as if melting under the painter's gaze'.[23]

Most of the film's budget was spent building this eerie fairy tale woodland across three sound stages at Shepperton Studios, and creating the illusion of huge trees soaring to a rarely-glimpsed sky. Due to the limited funds, the crew were forced to be much more imaginative in their approach; their 'forest' consisted of approximately a dozen three-dimensional trees with various branches, stumps and root structures on rollers so they could be moved around to create different spaces. The illusion of space was further enhanced by combining cut-outs, painted backgrounds and dioramas, bonsai trees and actual tree branches. According to Jordan, the look of the film formed an important part of the script, which was written to convey a heightened sense of reality. The director wanted everything to look irregular, with anthropomorphic trees and little cottages peering out from amongst dense woods. Carter, who was working on a novel during filming, visited the set several times and marvelled at the fairy tale land that had been created. She and Jordan had discussed building trees that resembled giant stiletto heels, but the low budget prevented him from doing so. While most of the film was shot in the studio, a couple of scenes were actually filmed on location: the exterior of the dreaming Rosaleen's family home, the garden where the wedding marquee is situated, and the interior of the little church in which the villagers gather for Sunday worship, an eighteenth-century church near Shepperton studios.

CASTING A FAIRY TALE

From his large-scale Hollywood blockbusters, to more personal art-house titles and myriad literary adaptations, Jordan has worked with a striking array of actors with varying degrees of experience: from non-actors to theatre actors to major Hollywood stars. To populate the peculiar pastoral landscapes of *The Company of Wolves*, Jordan wanted a very folkish, bucolic looking cast. For the part of Rosaleen, the film's protagonist and our conduit into the fairy tale dream-world where the narrative unfurls, he wanted a young, relatively inexperienced actress; someone who could act naturally. Aged 13 at the time of filming, *The Company of Wolves* was Sarah Patterson's first feature film role. Jordan praised her performance, particularly in the scenes in which she reacts to the amorous advances of the Huntsman, as she conveyed the right amount of attraction and horror. Despite her promising debut, Patterson only appeared in a few other films, including *Snow White* (1987), *Do I Love You?* (2002) and *Tick Tock Lullaby* (2007), before stepping out of the limelight entirely. Another cast member with very

Angela Lansbury as 'Granny' and Micha Bergese as 'The Huntsman'

limited acting experience was Micha Bergese in the role of the Huntsman. Jordan wanted someone with a physical, animalistic quality and when he was auditioning dancers from the worlds of ballet and contemporary movement, Jordan felt certain Bergese, a lithe performer with a background in mime, choreography and theatre, would bring something interesting to the role. Bergese later appeared in *Interview with the Vampire*. Jordan specifically wanted Angela Lansbury to play Granny and the actress was apparently very excited by the script. As Rosaleen comes to learn, Granny is not an entirely comforting figure, she possesses a somewhat dualistic nature perfectly conveyed by Lansbury's performance, which is equal parts benign and sinister. Jordan claimed he saw Granny as a humorous alter-ego of Angela Carter; a seductive storyteller pretending to tell cautionary tales about how one should behave and conduct oneself in society but is in fact exciting an illicit attraction for the forbidden.

For the part of the most wolfish creature of all, the Prince of Darkness himself, Jordan considered casting Andy Warhol. Woolley even visited Warhol in New York where he was recovering from being shot by radical feminist and SCUM manifesto scribe, Valerie Solanas. Due to his injuries Warhol was unable to travel, and budgetary restraints meant it was impossible for the crew to travel to New York for filming. The director eventually turned to Terence Stamp who, being a perfect gentleman and very fond of the script, accepted only the suit he wore in his scene as payment. This scene is one of the more bizarre in the film as it contains certain anachronistic elements – the car, the clothes – seemingly at odds with the context of the story. While wandering through the woods, a young man experiences the hypnotic seductiveness of evil when he encounters the Prince of Darkness in a chauffeur driven Rolls Royce. Jordan cast Patterson as the alluring chauffeur to pay homage to the films of Josef von Sternberg, particularly *Blonde Venus* (1932) and the duality of Marlene Dietrich's character. For the wolf-girl who emerges from the village well in the story Rosaleen tells the wounded Huntsman, Jordan cast avant-garde musician and visual artist Danielle Dax. Dax, who was apparently very affected by the role, delivers a captivating performance. The image of her, completely naked except for a tangled mane of hair, creeping through the shadows of the moonlit village, is an unforgettably striking one. Artificial tear ducts were placed beneath her eyes as Jordan wanted her to 'cry forever'.

FILMING

Once the cast had been assembled and the sets were built, filming began at Shepperton Studios just after Christmas in 1983 and lasted 8-10 weeks. Jordan and Woolley had no experience of shooting in a studio but appreciated being able to film within surroundings they could control. They had two full camera crews, many of whom had worked on large-scale films, but craved the opportunity to work on something more intimate. Cinematographer Bryan Loftus had worked on *2001: A Space Odyssey* (1968) in the effects team; editor Rodney Holland had been a sound editor on *Barry Lyndon* (1975) and *Don't Look Now* (1973); art director Stuart Rose worked on *Alien*; Elizabeth Waller was the costume designer on *For Your Eyes Only* (1981) and *Dr Who: The Robots of Death* (1977); and Sylvia Croft was a make-up artist on *Superman* (1978).

As each episode in the script demanded its own atmosphere and environment, sets needed to be rearranged. According to Jordan, each time the camera was moved it meant the sets had to be redressed and 'a microcosmic examination of the holes behind them' ensued.[24] Filming daytime scenes proved particularly difficult because the artificial nature of the sets was at risk of exposure from the bright lights. The director believed the sets looked best during the night-time scenes as he and Loftus were able to use

The wolf-girl and the well

light and shadow to suggest all manner of horrors. One of the main sets was the little village nestled in the dark heart of the forest. In the middle of it stands an ancient well; the same well glimpsed in the film's opening moments and from which the mysterious wolf-girl stealthily emerges in Rosaleen's story. The well holds a special place in folklore. It is a source of water, the availability of which proved essential for the positioning and survival of early communities. There were widely held beliefs throughout Europe that certain wells possessed mystical properties and that fairies lived beneath them. Other ancient beliefs denoted wells as entrances to a subterranean world populated by magical beings, not always benign. It was believed that those who drew water from these wells would be carried off to the world below, never to be seen again. Jordan said he wanted to create the impression the well reached down into unseen places, into the very bowels of the earth itself. He thought it so beautiful it cried out for more screen time, which he provided in the story Rosaleen tells her wounded suitor – one of the most hauntingly captivating, romantic and strange moments of the film – in which an inquisitive she-wolf emerges from its dark depths.

Another beautiful and oddly surreal sequence is also one of the most pivotal. Rosaleen, hiding from the clumsy advances of the amorous village boy, climbs a tall tree to survey the landscape and investigate the curious contents of a stork's nest. The wide shot of the forest with the figure of Rosaleen atop the tree, her scarlet shawl flying behind her in the wind, was created by placing a little doll on a miniature tree, surrounded by bonsai trees in front of a painted background. Jordan was adamant that everything that appeared on screen had to be created in tangible form; to have a 'different relationship to reality, the way cinema used to'.[25] He didn't want to use optical or digital effects, but real things that could be photographed. Even for the moments in which the moon can be glimpsed through frost-tinged cottage windows or grasping tree branches, Jordan wanted to create something real, and various moons – from icy slivers to 10ft circular discs – were built and hung from the studio ceiling. All the werewolf transformation sequences were realised with animatronics designed by Christopher Tucker (see **The Big Bad Wolf**). Less complicated effects included the moment when Granny is decapitated and her head shatters against the wall. This was created by taking a cast of Lansbury's face and moulding a replica in wax. Jordan cites this moment as one that reminds the audience that what they are seeing is a story. A story within a dream. It was filmed at 2000 frames per second, the same process used when filming the wolf as it bursts through the window in the dreaming girl's house.

Jordan had wanted to film a scene where the camera moves through the forest as the seasons change in one continuous, languid shot, but time and budget constraints didn't allow for it. Another moment from the original script which never made it into the film depicted a congregation of animals worshipping together in the church. As the priest reads from Isaiah chapter two, verses six to eight, Rosaleen is revealed to be sitting in the midst of a row of sheep with a wolf amongst them, a lion munching straw, a devoutly kneeling bear, an ox and a deer. The only moment from this scene to appear in the film is when a shower of spiders falls upon Rosaleen's lap from a large web-strewn chandelier above her head.

A somewhat more controversial omission from the original script was the ending. Carter had written the final scene to show Rosaleen waking up and jumping off her bed, diving into the floor which rippled like a pool of water. This moment was meant to convey the merging of the dream world with reality and while Jordan tried to achieve this, even going so far as to build a floor from wax, he was dissatisfied with the results. He and Carter believed the film should not end with the girl under threat; they wanted the climax to resemble a form of liberation, but the ending Jordan filmed creates a somewhat more ambiguous twist. Carter later confessed: 'I was furious about the ending. It wasn't scripted that way at all. I was out of the country in Australia when [Neil] shot the ending and he told me that it varied somewhat from the script. When I went to the screening I sat with Neil and I was enjoying the film very much and thinking it had turned out so well – just as I had hoped. Until the ending which I couldn't believe – I was so upset, I said "You've ruined it." He was apologetic […] I wish he had ended it right after the part where the white rose turns red.'[26]

SCORING A FAIRY TALE

The Company of Wolves features an evocative orchestral score equal parts haunting, romantic and eerie. When it came to scoring the film, Jordan turned to British composer George Fenton, who had written music for, amongst other titles, Gandhi (1982) and Walter (1982), which Jordan had greatly admired. Fenton, who cites the drama of church music as a major influence on his work, had three weeks to compose the music. The film was re-cut regularly, right up until he started composing the score, and then again before he began recording. When discussing the music, Jordan and Fenton concluded it should be lush, romantic, contain folksy, coming of age elements but still acknowledge the film's creepier aspects. To provide an appropriate sonic accompaniment for such a curious dream-world, Fenton turned to the work of Maurice Ravel for inspiration, particularly the ballet Daphnis et Chloé (1912), and when Jordan required music during the filming of the two wedding scenes Fenton used a piece of traditional Swedish folk music arranged for two violins.

Like so many others involved in the production, Fenton appreciated that The Company of Wolves wasn't easily classifiable and he wanted that to be reflected in the music. He worked closely with Jordan as he was keen to explore the relationship between electronic music and orchestral music, noting 'the grey area between sound and music where one stops and the other starts […] that's the most fascinating and unknown area in music'.[27] For the scene where the boy meets the devil in the forest, Fenton recorded himself breathing, dropped the pitch and mixed it with a solo bass to haunting effect. He claimed pieces such as this were written specifically to be recorded rather than performed, and that they should keep the audience from feeling too safe.

INFLUENCES

While he never directly references specific titles or texts, Jordan was keen to evoke various associations and obscure allusions to the worlds of art, cinema, literature, folklore and fairy tales. Given the nature of the story and the dream world in which it unfolds, Jordan wanted to play with dimensions and perspective in order to convey events from a child's point of view. He felt it was necessary to stir certain emotions and create atmospheres and imagery that would resonate with the viewer in a subconscious, connotative manner. Perhaps the most obvious influence, certainly in terms of narrative structure and thematic content, is Jaromil Jireš's *Valerie and Her Week of Wonders* (1970); indeed, Jordan's film was described by writer and film historian Michael Brooke as 'Valerie's most direct descendent'.[28] Based upon a surrealistic novel by the poet Vítězslav Nezval, Jireš's intoxicating film incorporates influences from Gothic literature, dream theory, fairy tales, Freudian symbolism and the work of Lewis Carroll. Exuding a dreamlike atmosphere, it tells of a young girl's macabre and fantastically erotic dreams instigated by her menarche, which begins as she steps out of a uterine carriage with a deep crimson interior. As Valerie (Jaroslava Schallerová) walks, drops of blood fall to the ground spattering pure white daisies, which she picks and brings to bed with her. Like *The Company of Wolves*, *Valerie* is not a probing psychological character study, it is highly allegorical and takes place within the dreams and fantasies of a young girl who occupies a purgatorial space between childhood and adulthood. The boundaries between dream and reality are fragile and fluid and in a state of constant flux. Many scenes occur during dawn or dusk, enhancing the notion that Valerie floats between worlds; night and day, rational and irrational, childhood and adulthood. Like Carter's werewolves, the various characters Valerie encounters throughout her reveries represent different aspects of adult sexuality; from the vampiric Tchoř, who inhabits a space between aggressive male sexuality and reassuring paternalistic love, to Valerie's mother/grandmother, who also turns out to be a vampire and represents lesbian desire and aggressive female sexuality. *Valerie and Her Week of Wonders* received a limited release in Britain and its premiere at the National Film Theatre was attended by Angela Carter, who apparently loved it.

Other cinematic works Jordan looked to for inspiration included *The Night of the Hunter* (1955), with its fairy tale-esque rite of passage narrative, Jean Cocteau's *Le belle et la bête* and the work of Michael Powell and Emeric Pressburger. *The Company of Wolves* shares a unique cinematic affinity with Powell and Pressburger 'whose richly textured visual and aural surreal and erotic worlds, such as the one created in the fairy-tale inspired *The Red Shoes* (1948), find a match in Jordan's sumptuous aesthetic'.[29] Further similarities between Jordan's film and *The Red Shoes* are apparent in the ways both titles draw attention to the artificiality of the medium of cinema itself; the deliberate staging, studio-bound sets, otherworldly atmospheres and purposeful theatricality of both titles resist any interpretation of realism. In his efforts to convey a sense of visual splendour and a pastoral, Constable-esque air, Jordan looked to the cinematic landscapes of *Gone to Earth* (1950), which tells of a young woman with a deep love for the wild creatures that dwell in the woods around her cottage, and her love for a reclusive nobleman whose inability to articulate his romantic needs relegates him to the peripheries of society. The stories within stories told throughout *The Company of Wolves* echo Powell and Pressburger's *A Canterbury Tale* (1944), the narrative of which is also propelled by thematically relevant stories told by various characters.

With its rich Gothic atmosphere and exploration of sexuality, *The Company of Wolves* is also indebted to the 'alternative history of British cinema'[30] represented by Hammer horror, as well as the shadowy worlds of silent horror cinema, specifically works of German Expressionism by Fritz Lang and F.W. Murnau. He also looked to Roger Corman's cycle of lush but minimally budgeted Edgar Allan Poe adaptations with their 'imaginative, horrific environments created through limited means, light and smoke'.[31] The scene in which the villagers brandish weapons and flaming torches to hunt down the wolf – a strangely misunderstood monster – evokes memories of old Universal horror films such as *Frankenstein* (1931) and *The Wolf Man* (1941). Jordan also admired Walerian Borowczyk's *The Beast* (1975), an erotic fantasy horror film concerned with savage sexual awakening and bestial desire. While *The Beast* fell foul of various censorship boards and was branded pornographic, Jordan thought it was as beautiful as it was disturbing. While not a werewolf film, the titular creature can be seen as a therianthropic rendering of base sexuality and primitive sexual urges. The female protagonist's various encounters with the beast in a secluded woodland demonstrate her exploration of her own sexuality, unshackling herself from the stifling conventions and repressions of society and delving into acts of sexual abandon.

WORKING WITH WOLVES

As well as Alaskan Malamutes, Alsatians and German Shepherds, various scenes throughout *The Company of Wolves* also feature real wolves. It was apparently very difficult to obtain the wolves, and just as difficult to secure insurance for them. Several were sourced from Scotland, but tragedy struck en route to Shepperton as one wolf killed and devoured another. Eventually a couple of other wolves were located and their handler was Teresa (Tsa) Palmer who, along with her late husband Roger, founded the UK Wolf Conservation Trust in 1995. Palmer began her cinematic wolf-handling career on *Legend of the Werewolf* (1975) before working on titles such as *Dracula* (1979) and *An American Werewolf in London*.

Jordan recalled needing great patience when filming the animals, as it took a long time 'to coax a wolf out of a well, over a bridge, or on to the bough of a tree'.[32] Palmer, who was on set with two wolves for approximately three weeks, also remembers how challenging it was:

> There were a number of scenes that I remember the filming of. The wolves, quite a lot of the time, seemed to be in a churchyard. It was always a question of the director saying, 'I'd like the wolves to come out of the well' and I'd say to him, 'Well, I'm not sure whether they will!' Wolves are quite surprising though, and they really rose to the occasion. I remember that most of the scenes we were filming were quite eerie, there were smoke machines and lighting. It was a question of putting the wolf in the well and getting it to go from A to B. They pretty much did everything that was required of them, plus much more. They were very socialised and because they were hand-raised and comfortable with most of what was going on they were fine. They did surprise us; instead of getting scared, they actually rather enjoyed the whole scenario.[33]

Jordan recalls the scene where the witch curses the wedding party as quite time consuming to film and cites this scene as one that people particularly remember because of its absurd and nightmarish qualities. To dress the wolves in eighteenth-century costumes the animals had to be tranquilised and asleep before they could be dressed. The crew then had to wait for the wolves to awaken before they could be filmed tearing the clothes off. It was an arduous process which took hours as the wolves,

'The wolf's eyes gleam, sometimes red, sometimes yellow...'

drowsy from the tranquiliser, kept falling asleep. Malamutes and Alsatians were also used in the scene, though they weren't as tricky to prepare and were simply dressed at the dining table and restrained until filming began. Much of the chaos of the transformations is glimpsed through a shattered mirror hanging in the marquee. The twisted, distorted reflections of the snarling guests conveys their depraved morality as their beastly natures erupt to the surface in a cacophony of bursting corsets, hirsute bosoms and bared fangs. Palmer recalls, 'When the director said he wanted the wolves to snarl, it's quite hard to get them to do that because if the wolf is snarling, it's because it's quite cross, and you don't really want to get them in a bad mood! So, you try to recreate the snarling by getting them to snap at a piece of food and try and get the shot that way.'[34] The incredibly striking imagery of the wolves' gleaming eyes peering out of the dark forest

The tenderness of wolves

was captured by director of effects photography Peter McDonald. By placing a light box in front of the camera lens and encasing pea-bulbs (miniature light bulbs frequently used in dollhouses) in a two-way mirror, he could throw the light towards the eyes of the wolves. According to Jordan, 'the wolf's eyes gleam, sometimes red, sometimes yellow. All of which shows me that imaginative fiction can sometimes have the precision of science'.[35]

The scene involving the use of a real wolf that caused the most tension on set, was the moment when Rosaleen comforts the wounded Huntsman after he has transformed from man to beast. An animal trainer with a gun was present on set, but the wolf was anything but aggressive, and demonstrated real affection towards Patterson, licking and nuzzling her. Jordan praised Patterson's performance and the delicate intimacy of the moment, and Palmer also recalls the bond shared between Patterson and her wolf, Queenie. 'I remember that really well. The wolves were reasonably young. When they become quite mature, over the age of four, they're not quite as malleable and they sometimes test the people they're working with. I think it helped that Sarah was fourteen. People who are a bit younger don't necessarily have that fear of wolves. Occasionally adult actors have been fearful and the wolves have picked up on it and growled, and then the actor becomes even more hesitant and nervous and it becomes a sort of self-defeating spiral. Sarah being fourteen thought this was all great, it was fun. I think that really helped. I've got several pictures of Sarah and Queenie. Sarah's face is literally on top of Queenie's, they're face to face. I was so happy and comfortable that Sarah was so in tune with Queenie and they got those wonderful shots and moments together.'[36]

In her short stories, Carter described wolves as 'carnivores incarnate', and while the presence of wolves on set may have been nerve-wracking for some of the cast and crew, Palmer claims that attitudes do change:

When you take wolves onto a film set, there's a lot of health and safety issues, people with guns in case anything happens, but usually by the end of the film the cast and crew are all patting the wolves and saying stuff like "hello dog!" Their perception of the wolves has completely changed. To start with I think people didn't really know that much about wolves. They were always very maligned and there were a lot of misconceptions about them. We all grow up with the tale of Red Riding Hood and the notion that wolves are vicious and are going to attack you. You've only got to think of the English language and how many times the word 'wolf' is used in a derogatory way; there are a lot of things in the English language that have that innuendo, that connotation. The other thing is that because wolves are quite nervous, they don't actually attack people, really. In the forty years or so I've been keeping wolves, I've luckily never been bitten. You just know where you are with them. You learn to read their signals and understand them. They're very charismatic. Slightly opportunist, too! If you like dogs, you might be sympathetic to wolves. Nowadays people have a different perception of wolves. They associate them with surviving in the wilderness. Their howl makes your backbone tingle. They're very special and I think it's nice to see people who have this inbuilt misconception that wolves are vicious come to think that wolves are actually okay. They're not the big bad beast you thought they were going to be.[37]

Palmer also noted that *The Company of Wolves*, and its portrayal of wolves and monsters, was quite different from many other films: 'Of all those werewolf films, *The Company of Wolves* didn't show them in a bad light. They had an aura about them in that film. They weren't necessarily bad, were they? They had that *je ne c'est quoi*; a slightly surreal quality to them.'[38]

FOOTNOTES

1. Rockett & Rockett (2003) p9
2. Zucker (2008) p1-3
3. ibid.
4. Zipes (2000a) p89
5. Frayling (2015) p45
6. Simpson, Helen (2006), *Femme fatale: Angela Carter's The Bloody Chamber.* https://www.theguardian.com/books/2006/jun/24/classics.angelacarter
7. Orenstein (2002) p167
8. Behind the Scenes Dossier, *The Company of Wolves* Special Edition DVD
9. Frayling (2015) p47
10. Zipes (2000a) p89-90
11. Carter, (2004) Frontispiece
12. Zucker (2013) pp40-41
13. Zucker (2013) p46
14. Zucker (2013) p45
15. Zucker (2013) p41
16. Bell (1997) p507
17. Jordan (1983) p51
18. Carter (1995) p111
19. Zucker (2013) p41
20. Producer Stephen Woolley on *The Company of Wolves*: http://www.bfi.org.uk/films-tv-people/4ce2ba0e97bc6
21. ibid.
22. Zucker (2013) p42
23. Zucker (2013) p43
24. Zucker (2013) p44
25. *The Company of Wolves* Special Edition DVD Commentary
26. Carroll, Rosemary (1986) *Interview with Angela Carter.* http://bombmagazine.org/article/821/angela-carter
27. Stoner, David (2013) *Interview with George Fenton*: http://www.runmovies.eu/george-fenton-on-the-company-of-wolves/
28. *Valerie and Her Week of Wonders*, filmed introduction by Michael Brooke, Second Run DVD
29. Rockett & Rockett (2003) p39
30. Cited in Rigby (2000) p239
31. *The Company of Wolves* Special Edition DVD Commentary
32. Zucker (2013) p44

33. Telephone interview with author (10th March, 2016)

34. ibid.

35. Zucker (2013) pg 40

36. Telephone interview with author (10th March, 2016)

37. ibid.

38. ibid.

CHAPTER TWO: TELLING TALES

'As children, we need monsters to instruct us in the ways of the world.'
Bruno Bettelheim

Fairy tales, folklore and the art of (oral) storytelling are all woven into the very fabric of *The Company of Wolves*. The film's fragmented narrative structure, which exists within the dreams of a sleeping adolescent girl, is comprised of stories told to her dream-self by her Granny, and later, by tales the girl herself tells others. Each of the stories conveys a specific message to the listener, and to the audience; from Granny's tale of an unfortunate local girl who unwittingly marries a werewolf, which speaks of Granny's mistrust of men, to Rosaleen's tale of a wounded wolf-girl, which tells of Rosaleen's curiosity and gradual acceptance of her own maturing sexuality. In their exploration of the power of narrative and storytelling, and the myriad ways in which the same stories can convey different meanings to different listeners, Jordan and Carter utilise the rich language and imagery of folk and fairy tales to explore notions of identity and gender, and how such notions are culturally constructed and perpetuated. *The Company of Wolves* plays with the form of the fairy tale and its ideas regarding initiation, redemption and personal and social progress, to explore the changes and uncertainties of growing up; though it stops short of offering a stable and happy resolution. Throughout the process of adapting the film, Carter and Jordan emphasised the significance of the tellers and the listeners of stories and how each embellishes and interprets the stories they tell and hear in different ways.

In order to more fully understand Jordan and Carter's process of demythologising culturally constructed notions of gender and identity by retelling the very fairy tales that helped establish such notions, it is necessary to look at the history and evolution of folk and fairy tales. This chapter will explore the role played by such tales in conditioning communities, and how certain tales were repurposed through literary adaptations to educate and instruct different types of audiences.

Folk and fairy tales have existed for as long as mankind and they have provided figurative commentaries on the customs of the societies in which they are told. They tell of how the endeavours of certain people or groups of people can bring about the possibility of happiness for other individuals and their communities. While they offer hope to the downtrodden, they don't all have happy endings; some also offer warnings and promise dire consequences for certain actions and behaviour. These tales work on a subconscious level to teach us about ourselves and the world we inhabit. They are stories which frequently offer a cautionary morality, warning and preparing listeners and readers for the trials and tribulations they will face and ultimately strive to overcome throughout their lives. The literary fairy tales we're familiar with today, and the oral folk tales upon which they are frequently based are grounded in history. They emanate from 'specific struggles to humanize bestial barbaric forces that have terrorized our minds and communities in concrete ways'.[1] Variations of familiar tales exist in cultures throughout the world; the same stories told in different ways. The universality of these stories speaks of the common plights experienced by people everywhere. According to folk and fairy tale scholar Jack Zipes, 'human beings, as a species, have the same basic struggles and work through a lot of the same troubles in family life and society. These struggles are reflected in tales told by common people, and not so common people, and they all, to a certain extent, relate to the fact that we as a species have the same problems'.[2]

Folk and fairy tales remain a relevant and powerful form of storytelling because of their ability to be constantly reinterpreted and retold, making them relatable for generation after generation. The ways in which these tales can be reworked and retold to address certain changes and values in society is especially evident in Carter's collection of reinterpreted fairy tales, *The Bloody Chamber*. When Carter rewrote these tales, she was mounting a critique of relations between the sexes and culturally constructed gender roles in patriarchal society, and the role that folk and fairy stories has played in establishing and prolonging these ideas. She deliberately chose stories that were violently sexual in their subject matter and by reinterpreting them she purposefully drew out certain latent content. Throughout the tales, Carter foregrounds the performance of storytelling and frequently uses specific language to directly address the reader. She continued to explore the power of storytelling, and the way knowledge and customs are orally transmitted when she adapted several of the stories for radio. When she and Jordan came to adapt the stories for film, they worked largely from the radio adaptation, again focusing on the significance of the relationship between storyteller and listener. By utilising this approach, Jordan and Carter echoed the fluidity of the original tales and how those tales evolve over time. With each retelling, ideologies and artistic preferences change, creating a ripple effect that results in more and more changes, meaning it becomes increasingly impossible to trace tales back to an original source.

According to Zucker, the use of folk and fairy tales in *The Company of Wolves* 'is not a correction or parody of their supposedly outdated values; rather, [Jordan] investigates what it means to listen to fairy tales, what it means to trust narrative and what it means to follow their paths'.[3] Carter and Jordan also rely upon the familiarity and ubiquity of these tales and the motifs and imagery contained within them. As Zipes explains 'One knows [these fairy tales], and one loves them because they have been absorbed in a habitual way. And one takes pleasure in them without having any reason'.[4] According to Jordan, this pleasure and habitual familiarity was an important part of the writing process, explaining 'we tried to let images and types of stories come to us in an associative way, and follow them for the pleasure of it. I think the meaning emerges from the pleasure, rather than in any straight-forward interpretive way [...] When I was a kid, the pleasure I got from Disney films, or from *Night of the Hunter* or *The Wizard of Oz*, was more to do with recognition than interpretation'.[5]

STORIES OF THE COMMON FOLK

Despite frequent interchangeability, there are distinct differences, etymologies and meanings between folk and fairy tales. Folk tales are probably as old as mankind and usually derive from oral traditions. To deduce that folkloric tradition was exclusively oral however, would be an over-generalisation. It is frequently impossible to separate written from oral versions because as tales were told and re-told and written and re-written, they transformed and even combined with other tales or motifs, both printed *and* oral. Originally told by adults for adults, the tales were passed on through spoken word and were closely connected to the customs and beliefs of the communities in which they were told. Such tales helped establish a sense of identity and community spirit as they instructed, warned and entertained listeners. Land labourers and household servants would have told such tales to alleviate the monotony of their daily work. These tales would have had rowdy, dramatic narratives containing outrageous comedy, melodrama and violence. Certain tales also featured wondrous, sometimes supernatural elements, and many would later serve as the basis for literary fairy tales.

Folk and fairy tales are relics of former cultural traditions that demonstrate how 'humans throughout the world invent and use stories in very similar ways to expose and articulate common problems and struggles as well as their wishes to overcome them'.[6] By using metaphors understandable and accessible to the reader/listener, folk and fairy tales provide hope that negative personal, social and political situations can change for the better, that evil can be defeated. According to Zipes the reason these tales have been so popular and endured for so long is because of their reassurance: 'They offer counter worlds to our real world; counter worlds in which there is always justice. The nasty queens and the nasty kings are always punished by the "small" people in fairy tales and folk tales; those who come from the lower classes and generally strive to better their situation, and quite often succeed in doing so. There are some fairy tales that end tragically, but for the most part they end on a note that provides happiness to the people that have been struggling, and they also provide social justice. You can understand why people want to escape into the worlds of fairy tales, because they can see alternatives to the bleak conditions in which we're living today'.[7] The urge to share stories and tell of experiences relevant in our lives in order to aid the listener to find ways to improve his/her situation, is universal. Zipes also suggests, 'No tale is ever told for the first time, but every tale is memetically disseminated and retained in our memory to enable us to navigate our way through the tons of messages and stories that bombard our lives from the day we are born'.[8]

Towards the end of the eighteenth century, attitudes towards history and national identity in Europe began to change due to a rise in education, literacy and the expansion of universities and academic libraries. This led to the renewed appreciation of folk and fairy tales, legends, myths, practices and superstitions from the past and how they fed into and informed popular culture. With the formation of folklore societies, the study of the stories of the common man became validated and regarded as an intellectual discipline. Folklore emerged as a legitimate field of study throughout Europe as folklorists sought to understand their present by collecting common tales and practices from the past. While there is no widespread agreement on a definition, the term 'folklore' was coined by English antiquarian William John Thoms in August 1846 in a letter he wrote to The Athenaeum, a magazine 'catering to the intellectually curious'.[9]

Thoms suggested the term 'folklore' be used instead of 'popular antiquities', which had formerly been used to refer to the study of culturally significant tales, practices, customs and values.

Folk tales from the oral tradition were gathered, written down and published to ensure they would not expire. Folklorists observed the ways in which people from different classes and communities verbally transmitted accepted beliefs and practices through narrative storytelling. At the forefront of this movement were the Brothers Grimm who, while still in their teens and ensconced in studies at the university of Marburg, were highly influential as compilers and preservers of folk stories. The Grimms believed the 'most natural and pure forms of culture – those which had held communities together – were linguistic and were to be located in the past'.[10] They held that the study of such tales and customs could not only be used to gain an understanding of the past, but also of the present. The brothers sought to trace the evolution of cultural standards and attitudes through the language, customs and rituals of the common people who conveyed their experiences through storytelling. They believed this to be an educational endeavour and soon came to realise that such tales and folk traditions existed and held a great deal of relevance in all cultures, and that by passing on these stories, certain traditions throughout the world were upheld and perpetuated. In the preface of the first edition of *Children's & Household Tales* (1812) the Grimms noted, 'We wanted not merely to serve the history of [the tales] with our collection. It was our intention at the same time to bring out the living aspect in these tales so that it has an effect and can provide pleasure for whomever it could, and consequently the tales could become an actual educational manual'.[11]

In the early twentieth century, attempts were made to categorise different types of tales, resulting in the publication of the Aarne-Thompson tale-type index. Developed by Finnish folklorist Antti Aarne, and later revised by American folklorist Stith Thompson, the index is used to classify folk and fairy tales, and catalogues several thousand basic plots upon which countless European and Near Eastern storytellers built their tales.

LITERARY FAIRY TALES

Tales continued to be told, retold and written down, changing and evolving to embrace and demonstrate social changes, creating a rich tapestry of oral and written histories and traditions. As more of these tales were recorded they began to establish their own conventions, motifs, characters and plots, based largely on those developed in the oral tradition but altered to appeal to a mainly aristocratic readership. Until they received courtly approval, however, the resulting translations of these folk tales were often dismissed as a literary form by bourgeois classes. Middle class writers gradually transformed the common folk tales told to them by their governesses and servants into 'high art'. While many critics claim the lower classes were excluded from the formation of this evolving literary tradition, it was their 'material, tone, style, and beliefs'[12] that were incorporated into what began to constitute the genre of the literary fairy tale, which folk narrative scholars refer to as 'magic tales'. The term 'fairy tale' first appeared in the title of Mme Marie-Catherine d'Aulnoy's 1697 collection of tales. It can refer to either a category of oral folk tale containing wondrous, supernatural elements, or a translation of a form of oral narrative fashionable in the French Court of the late seventeenth century, as well as a literary genre which may or may not be based on oral tradition.

As the oral tales were recorded, changes were made to their tone and content for various reasons. Certain changes were at the behest of publishers who perhaps initially considered fairy tales trivial and associated them with peasant superstitions. Other changes occurred when dialects were moderated, explicit content was toned down and when authors imposed their own artistic preferences and moral inclinations. The Grimms, for example, held motherhood to be sacred and the various wicked step-mothers that populate their tales were actually biological mothers in the original folk tales. The Grimms also felt it was important to be reflective of social relevance and at this time many women died in childbirth and were replaced by younger step-mothers, often jealous of older stepdaughters. When they realised for various reasons they couldn't faithfully record the tales as told by the tellers, the Grimms gradually embellished them and it is possible to trace the changes and newly evolving tales through each edition of their work. The tales recorded in the early editions retained a raw, authentic tone, while evident changes in later versions – including translated dialects, more descriptive language and the addition of religious sentiment – demonstrate attempts to increase dramatic license and reflect changing social realities. As such, their tales, and the changes made to them can be seen as revealing timely concerns such as familial and generational conflicts, the mistreatment of the young and the poor, the persecution of women, and the corruption and abuse of political power.

It is generally assumed fairy tales were first created for children and are largely the domain of children, but Zipes insists 'nothing could be further from the truth'.[13] While these tales would later be used to civilise children, offering social indoctrination through anxiety-provoking effects and positive/negative reinforcement, it wasn't until the late nineteenth century that the tales were made appropriate for children by the likes of Edgar Taylor, who was the first to translate the tales of the Brothers Grimm into English. While the Grimms didn't deny that children should hear them or read them, according to Zipes their tales were not written specifically for children, 'they were for a wider audience, particularly adults. They even had scholarly notes in the first editions. If one reads the Grimms' tales carefully, you'll see that they really were not intended for children'.[14] Once the tales had been collected and moderated in the recording process, they gradually came to be used to reinforce what was deemed to be socially and morally acceptable to middle class and bourgeois readers. As educated writers continued to appropriate oral folk tales and rewrite their literary counterparts, they increasingly converted the stories to a type of literary discourse about values and manners so aristocratic children would become civilised according to the social codes of the time. French fairy tale writers took the genre very seriously and endeavoured to incorporate into their narrative structures the ideas, norms and values they considered worthy of emulation for young, or indeed, adult readers. Charles Perrault was one such writer, and he not only refined fairy tales to be told in courtly circles, but wrote them specifically to civilise and instruct bourgeois children in the roles he believed they should play in society (See **Red Hoods, Dark Woods**).

While such tales have assumed different forms and tones throughout history, revealing and perpetuating particular beliefs and traditions as they've been told and retold by each generation, they have also assumed immense relevance throughout all cultures, revealing their universality. The widespread and enduring popularity of these tales suggests that they address certain issues that have a 'significant social function – whether critical, conservative, compensatory, or therapeutic'.[15] Such tales 'register an effort on the part of both women and men to develop maps for coping with personal anxieties, family conflicts, social frictions, and the myriad frustrations of everyday life'.[16] Pondering the timeless relevance of folk and fairy tales, Zipes notes that 'wherever tales still exist, they continue to live in a way that nobody contemplates whether they are good or bad, poetic or crude […] People die away while the tales persist'.[17]

FOOTNOTES

1.   Zipes (2007) pp1-2
2.   Gracey, James (2012) *A Fairy Tale Influence – Interview with Jack Zipes* http://www.exquisiteterror.com/a-fairy-tale-influence
3.   Zucker (2008) pp4-5
4.   Tatar (1999) xx
5.   Zucker (2013) p47
6.   Zipes (2013) xxxii
7.   Gracey, James (2012) *A Fairy Tale Influence – Interview with Jack Zipes* http://www.exquisiteterror.com/a-fairy-tale-influence
8.   Zipes (2015) p32
9.   Dorson (1982) pg 1
10.   Zipes (2013) xix
11.   Zipes (2013) xx
12.   Zipes (2007) p3
13.   Zipes (2007) p1
14.   Gracey, James (2012) *A Fairy Tale Influence – Interview with Jack Zipes* http://www.exquisiteterror.com/a-fairy-tale-influence
15.   Tatar (1999) xi
16.   ibid.
17.   Tatar (1999) xx

CHAPTER THREE: RED HOODS, DARK WOODS

'Surely the most primitive and obvious werewolf legend of all, accepted from the earliest days of our dawning intelligence, is the tale of Little Red Riding Hood.'
Gerald Biss, *The Door of the Unreal* (1919)

Of all the fairy tales ever told, the tale of Little Red Riding Hood is one of the most enduring and provocative. The plight of the red-hooded girl who encounters a ravenous wolf as she wanders cautiously through the deep, dark woods on an errand to her Granny's cottage has haunted popular culture for centuries. From its apparent origins as a 'bildungsroman' (coming of age story) of mischievous initiation, through its literary adaptations as a cautionary, morally conservative fairy tale and its myriad reinterpretations by contemporary writers and film-makers, Red Riding Hood has been told and re-told for centuries; its meaning interpreted and reinterpreted to reflect changing social values and attitudes. Zipes suggests the story of Red Riding Hood is reflective of the ways in which oral and literary traditions have interacted to create differing versions of the same incident: the violation and rape of a young girl when she ventures alone through the forest. When Angela Carter re-wrote Red Riding Hood for *The Bloody Chamber*, she transformed it into a critique of prior literary versions, particularly Charles Perrault's, and the conservative morality they proffered that strongly suggested 'little girls want and cause their own rape'.[1] Carter empowered her heroine by giving her a strong sense of her own sexual awareness.

All of the stories told by different characters within the narrative of *The Company of Wolves* lead to one particular moment (Rosaleen's encounter with the lycanthropic Huntsman in the woods) and according to Jordan are essentially 'an elaborate preparation for the central story, which is of course, Little Red Riding Hood [...] Once the film reaches these moments there's a perverse satisfaction in treading familiar territory'.[2] In keeping with the film's dreamlike atmosphere these moments are at once familiar yet unfamiliar as Carter and Jordan toy with expectations and subvert ideas regarding gender roles and happy endings. As mentioned in the previous chapter, folk and fairy tales were used to civilise listeners and readers in the ways of their communities and convey to them an understanding of acceptable conduct and behaviour. This was frequently achieved through the positive and negative reinforcements contained in the tales. The stories Rosaleen is told by her Granny are an attempt by the old woman to make the girl behave in a certain way, to make her fear men and suppress her sexuality. They only serve to excite the girl's curiosity, however, and the story culminates in her (off-screen) transformation into a wolf; a bittersweet ending as she finally obtains experience and freedom, but in doing so becomes lost to her family. Though she can now run free with her lover in the woods she does so as an outcast, as a wolf in woman's clothing. This seems to speak of the sacrifices that must be made and the difficulties that must be overcome in quests of self-discovery.

Into the woods

While fairy tales can be retold and reinterpreted in ways so varied it seems they often don't have a single, unambiguous meaning, the story of Red Riding Hood is generally regarded as one of the most effective expressions of sexual curiosity and the ultimate loss of innocence. Indeed, certain connotative, Eden-esque imagery throughout *The Company of Wolves* alludes to temptation, seduction and an inevitable fall from grace. On numerous occasions Rosaleen's journeys through the forest are observed by large snakes coiled around outstretched branches, and glistening apples – the fruit of temptation – are frequently glimpsed. Elsewhere, Rosaleen is espied observing a spider, silently spinning a silken web, and a moth fluttering dangerously close to a softly burning candle.

THE EVOLUTION OF A TALE

It is believed the tale of Red Riding Hood has an ancient history and variations of it have existed in many cultures. While it is impossible to trace its origins, folklorists suggest it first emerged in Africa or Asia. In its most basic form it is a tale of good vs. evil, light vs. dark: Red's cloak represents the sun/daylight, and the wolf, darkness/night. The swallowing of the girl by the wolf, and her subsequent re-emerging from his stomach (as she does in many versions) speaks of the notion of rebirth. In order to gain knowledge and experience and be 'reborn', one must undergo hardship, an idea as old as mankind and echoed in myths and tales throughout the world. From Fenrir devouring the sun in Norse mythology, the Biblical tale of Jonah and the whale, and the Greek legend of Cronos gobbling up his own children, the fear of being devoured is ancient and universal. It is echoed throughout many fairy tales, including Hansel and Gretel, the Seven Little Goats and Tom Thumb.

It is not clear when or how significant motifs such as the red hood, the wolf (in certain versions it was a werewolf or a flesh-eating ogre or some other geographically relevant monster), and the suggestion of the girl's sexual violation – evident in many Greco-Roman myths – were added to the basic structure of the tale. As red is the colour of blood it has long been associated with sacrifice, passion, danger and sexuality. Its use in the tale connotes not only the burgeoning sexuality of the girl, but the sexual violence to which the tale alludes. The wolf was perhaps introduced when the tale reached Europe because it was the most widespread carnivore in the Northern Hemisphere and posed a real threat to man. According to Bruno Bettelheim, whose *Uses of Enchantment* (1976) explores the psychology of fairy tales through a distinctly Freudian lens, the tale of Red Riding Hood speaks of 'human passions, oral greediness, aggression, and pubertal sexual desires'.[3] Maria Tatar claims that Charles Perrault was the first to add the motif of the red hood,[4] and this was most likely to underline the sexual connotations of the tale. However, Bettelheim references a Latin story, 'Fecunda ratis' (1023) attributed to Egbert of Lièges, which concerned 'a little girl [...] found in the company of wolves; the girl wears a red cover of great importance to her, and scholars tell that this cover was a red cap. Here, then, six centuries or more before Perrault's story, we find some basic elements of Little Red Riding Hood: a little girl with a red cap, the company of wolves, a child being swallowed alive who returns unharmed, and a stone put in place of the child'.[5] It was actually in this footnote of Bettelheim's book that Carter found the title for her reinterpretation of Red Riding Hood. The tale described by Bettelheim also echoes throughout Carter's story 'Wolf-Alice' and the excised tale told by the Huntsman in an early draft of the screenplay for *The Company of Wolves*, in which a young girl is raised by wolves, coming of age and sexual awareness outside the confines of society.

According to Zipes, versions of Red Riding Hood were told in Italy during the fourteenth century, including 'La finta nonna' ('The False Grandmother'),[6] while other versions existed in France in the tenth century. French folklorists such as Yvonne Verdier, Paul Delarue and Charles Joisten claimed the tale and variations of it were told amongst women in sewing circles during the early seventeenth century in the south of France and north of Italy. According to Willem de Blécourt, the French 'Story of Grandmother', recorded in Nièvre around 1885, is generally believed to resemble a similar tale that could have inspired Perrault two hundred years earlier.[7]

This tale tells of a young peasant woman who journeys through the woods to take food to her ailing grandmother. In the woods, she encounters a werewolf at a crossroads – a place long associated with important decisions. It should be noted that at this time belief in werewolves was rife throughout Europe – they were seen as a very real threat to rural communities. The werewolf asks the young woman whether she intends to take 'the path of the pins or the path of the needles?' This odd question, which makes sense if the tale was told amongst sewing circles, relates to needlework apprenticeships that young girls would have undertaken; the story was most likely told to them by older, more experienced women. As it is easier to fasten things together with pins, and takes much more time and attention to sew with needles, the question perhaps relates to her approach to her work as a seamstress: would she take the path of the needles and work hard, or would she just take short cuts and pin everything together without thinking of the future? When he has asked the question, the werewolf bounds through the woods to the Grandmother's house where he kills and eats her. He offers the leftover flesh and blood to the granddaughter when she eventually arrives and then invites the girl to get into bed with him, suggesting she throw her clothes in the fire as she won't be needing them anymore. This implies he is going to devour her, either literally or sexually. When the girl slips between the sheets with the werewolf she asks him several questions relating to his physical aspects and receives brief, sinister responses, culminating in the familiar 'All the better to eat you with, my dear.' The quick-witted girl realises the werewolf's intentions and declares she must first relieve herself, but refuses to do so in the bed, as the werewolf suggests. She claims that if he can't trust her to not runaway, he should tie a rope around her ankle. Once outside, she removes the rope, ties it to a tree and runs home through the forest. When he realises she has escaped, the werewolf gives chase and only catches up with her in time to have her front door slammed firmly shut in his face.

Reputedly earlier versions of the tale such as this one appear to convey a sense of initiation that is apparently reflective of an old French peasant tradition, the practice of which involved figuratively 'losing' oneself in the wild to attain experience, a deeper sense of self-awareness and understanding of the wider world. As German author and anthropologist Hans Peter Duerr explains: 'In the archaic mentality, the fence, the hedge, which separated the realm of wilderness from that of civilisation did not represent limits which were unsurpassable. On the contrary, this fence was even torn down at certain times. People who wanted to live within the fence with awareness had to leave this enclosure at least once in their lifetime. They had to have roamed the woods as wolves or "wild persons." That is, to put in more modern terms; they had to have experienced the wilderness in themselves, their animal nature. For their "cultural nature" was only one side of their being, bound by fate to the animal-like *fylgja*, which became invisible to those people who went beyond the fence and abandoned themselves to their 'second face'.[8] Zipes suggests this tradition was especially associated with individuals in rural communities accused of witchcraft and werewolfism: individuals not bound by social conformity and therefore regarded as outsiders by the moral majority. By temporarily abandoning herself to the werewolf and subsequently thwarting his plans to devour her, Red Riding Hood 'looks death in the eye so she may live'[9] and for a brief moment she inhabits the space between civilisation and the wilderness; the wilderness of sensuality, carnality and abandon. She rejects socially constructed traditions relating to her pre-assigned role in society. When she returns home, she is no longer a young girl, but a woman of knowledge, experience and most importantly, self-awareness.

CHARLES PERRAULT & LESSONS LEARNED

The literary history of Red Riding Hood begins in 1697 with the publication of Charles Perrault's 'Le Petit Chaperon Rouge'. When he wrote 'Le Petit Chaperon Rouge', Perrault's intention was to instil a specific moral lesson – 'girls who invite strange men into their parlours deserve what they get'[10] – in bourgeois readers/listeners and his adaptation emphasises the sexual seduction of the girl by the wolf. While sexuality is never explicitly mentioned, the way in which it is implied enables the reader/listener to understand what is meant. Perrault makes this metaphor even more obvious when the wolf replies to Red Riding Hood's observation about his large arms, saying 'all the better to *embrace* you'. When the girl does nothing to save herself in Perrault's tale, Bettelheim claims it is because she is either 'stupid' and unaware of the danger she is in, or, perhaps more significantly given Perrault's obvious metaphor, because she *wants* to be seduced. Certain commentators have suggested the wolf in the tale is not just a 'male seducer' but is representative of asocial and animalistic tendencies within all of us, and it is not only important to understand the nature of the wolf, but what makes him attractive to us. In the words of Bettelheim 'if there were not something in us that likes the big bad wolf, he would have no power over us'.[11] The word 'wolf' has become synonymous with predatory lotharios and Red Riding Hood operates so successfully as a fable of sexual warning because, as Glen Duncan notes, it concedes 'the power of the [wolf's] charm'.[12] Bettelheim claims Gustav Doré's illustration expresses these same underlying feelings – the girl is 'beset by powerful ambivalent feelings as she looks at the wolf resting beside her'.[13] She is intrigued and curious, like Rosaleen, and makes no attempt to leave the bed. As Djuna Barnes suggests, 'Children know something they can't tell; they like Red Riding Hood and the wolf in bed'.[14] By giving expression to her fancy the girl in Perrault's story brings about her own downfall and that of her grandmother. She is not rescued by a woodsman nor does she have the sense to save herself as she did in the earlier oral tales. Perrault wanted to provide young female readers/listeners with a certain model of behaviour and by the girl's negative example the reader/listener learns how a 'good girl' should behave. She must never talk to strangers, she must exercise restraint and suppress her sexuality or else she will suffer dire consequences. To further emphasise his intention Perrault concludes his tale, after Red Riding Hood's gory demise, with a little verse which blatantly spells out the moral he wished to imbue:

Rosaleen meets the Huntsman

'Not all wolves are exactly the same […] But watch out if you haven't learned that tame wolves are the most dangerous of all.' In other words, and as Carter so poetically put it, 'Sweetest tongue has sharpest tooth.'

Bettelheim attributes the enduring popularity of Little Red Riding Hood and its reputation as a morally conservative fable of sexual warning to Perrault's adaptation. Most critics agree that by Perrault's hand, the tale changed from a tale warning girls of the dangers of predators, to warning them against their own sexual desires. If Perrault was indeed familiar with the likes of the 'Story of Grandmother', or indeed early variations of it, his adaptation transformed it into a tale in which a spoiled and naïve young girl of bourgeois heritage 'pays for her stupidity and is violated in the end'.[15] Tatar suggests that in earlier tales such as the 'Story of Grandmother', Red Riding Hood assumes the figure of trickster, as she performs a striptease for the wolf, gets into bed with him, and then cunningly escapes.[16] Zipes claims the peasant girl in these earlier tales is perceptive, brave and 'for the most part […] proves that she can fend for herself'[17] – a very different girl from the one who is gobbled up in Perrault's tale and one much more in keeping with Carter's interpretation of the tale.

It has been suggested Perrault would have removed the more vulgar aspects of such tales, particularly the unwitting acts of cannibalism and references to the girl relieving herself, as he was writing for the bourgeois audiences of the Palace of Versailles and as such, prettified his adaptations. However, Willem de Blécourt claims it is unlikely that Perrault adapted the 'Story of Grandmother' because it would indicate that the elements he allegedly excised would have remained unaltered throughout years of being retold, which was highly unlikely because every storyteller augments and embellishes the tales they tell. Zipes argues that Perrault *would* have been familiar with tales that emanated from sewing circles in the south of France and the north of Italy and that 'such a symbolic ritual expressed in the original folk tale about a strong young woman confused and irritated Perrault. His hostility toward the pagan folk tradition and fear of women were exhibited in all his tales'.[18] While de Blécourt suggests Perrault may well have just wanted to tell his own 'conte du loup' (wolf tale) 'modernised by elaborating on the saying avoir vu un loup (to have seen a wolf), which, when applied to a girl, meant that she had lost her innocence',[19] he points to another story called 'The Werewolf Husband' as a possible inspiration for Perrault. This tale tells of a man who attacks his wife when he turns into a wolf. When he transforms back into a man, he is identified as the murderer because of the threads of her clothing stuck between his teeth. Zipes claims that Perrault would also have been familiar with a specific werewolf trial that took place in his mother's home town of Tourine[20] and this may have served as further inspiration.

A number of scholars have echoed claims that because of the way in which Perrault adapted the tale for literary purposes, he effectively robbed it of its original meaning. Bettelheim claimed that the various layers of meaning in fairy tales should become clear to the child as it grows up, and suggested this process changes a story the child has heard into something the child partially creates and therefore actually learns from. The changes made to the tale by Perrault therefore meant, in Bettelheim's opinion, it lost much of its appeal because it was so obvious that his wolf was a metaphor and left little to the imagination of the reader/listener. According to Bettelheim, when meanings such as this are so detailed in fairy tales, it robs the value of the tale for the child. Zipes argues Perrault 'totally corrupted the perspective and import of the warning tale'[21] and instead of warning girls of the dangers of predators, Perrault warns them against exploring their own sexual desires. The oral folk tales featured a highly Carter-esque heroine who displayed 'a natural, relaxed attitude toward her body and sex and meets the challenge of a would-be seducer'.[22] This brave peasant girl who fends for herself, displaying traits such as courage and wit, becomes a helpless, spoilt bourgeois girl, delicate and naïve and punished for her inability to control herself. Tatar also argued the story lost more than it gained in Perrault's version as it changed from 'adult oral entertainment to literary fare for children',[23] and Erich Fromm interprets it as the 'expression of a deep antagonism against men and sex'.[24] While Bettelheim claimed that Perrault changed Red Riding Hood into a figure the reader/listener cannot identify with because she is a 'fallen woman', others suggest that the enduring popularity of the tale and its protagonist is because of her fallibility; the heroine is *not* perfect, and this makes her relatable. She is curious and makes mistakes. She is naïve and is tempted. In Perrault's version, however, this imperfection is what damns her.

As a tale of initiation and rite of passage, Red Riding Hood also speaks of the struggles and conflicts between younger and older generations. The younger generation must learn from their elders and prove themselves worthy of following in the footsteps of those who have gone before. Some commentators suggest that Red Riding Hood tells the wolf exactly where her grandmother lives as a subconscious act of rebellion; she knows that the wolf will eat her grandmother, therefore eliminating an obstacle from the girl's road to adulthood. She will be free to make her own choices now that she feels ready to. When Rosaleen's sister Alice is hunted down and devoured by the wolves, it can be read as Rosaleen subconsciously eliminating her competition; effectively removing 'the first obstacle to her own maturation and sexual fulfilment'.[25] According to Rockett and Rockett, in order for the younger girl to resolve her oedipal journey, she must 'displace the older, more sexually attractive competition'.[26] In Carter's short story 'The Werewolf', when Red discovers her Granny is a werewolf she alerts the neighbours who stone the old woman to death. The story ends thus: *Now the child lived in her grandmother's house; she prospered.*[27] When Rosaleen and Granny visit Alice's grave, and Granny presents Rosaleen with a red shawl, the priest tells them that 'someone's got to cut away the old wood. Even evergreens need pruning.' What he seems to allude to is that one way or another the older generation need to make way for the younger generation and, in true fairy tale fashion, allow the 'absence created through the death of the grandmother or eldest daughter [to be] filled by the next in line'.[28] The cape that Granny gives Rosaleen is an invitation into adulthood. Rockett and Rockett suggest it 'doubles as sexual invitation', its red fabric 'the colour of passion and of menses, the blood she must spill to live and become a woman'.[29] Bettelheim suggests the red cape given to the girl by her grandmother represents a premature transfer of sexual attractiveness from the grandmother to the girl, who is too young to understand what it symbolises and what her wearing of it implies. He goes on to opine that the danger the girl finds herself in stems from her developing sexuality, suggesting premature sexuality is a regressive experience, arousing all that is primitive and all that threatens to overwhelm and swallow us up.

After Perrault's tale had been translated into various European languages, other writers used it as a template, introducing new elements. Ludwig Tieck published 'The Life & Death of Little Red Cap' in 1800 and introduced the figure of the heroic huntsman who saves her life. Christian Schneller's version in 1867 takes a turn for the visceral as the wolf becomes an ogre who replaces the latch on Granny's door with the poor woman's entrails and puts her blood, teeth and jaws in the kitchen cupboard.

In 1812 the Brothers Grimm wrote 'Rotkäppchen' (Little Red Cap) and not only retained the figure of the huntsman introduced by Tieck and the salvation of Red Riding Hood, but actually afforded Red the opportunity to redeem herself and demonstrate a more proactive role. When she is cut free from the stomach of the wolf it is *she* who gathers the large stones to place in the opened belly as she believes that to feel safe again, she must 'do away with the seducer'[30] herself. The Grimms also added an extended conclusion depicting Red Riding Hood's encounter with another wolf, and in doing so strongly reiterate how important it is to learn from past mistakes. When the girl encounters the second wolf she realises she is ill-equipped to deal with its advances and goes straight to her grandmother, who instructs the girl what to do. They fill a trough with water and drown the wolf. According to Bettelheim: 'The child thus needs to form a strong working alliance with the parent of the same sex, so that through identification with the parent and conscious learning from him, the child will grow successfully into an adult.'[31] For the girl to transcend the boundaries of childhood into the realms of adulthood and experience, it was necessary for her to stray from the path. Wilhelm Grimm would later make minor but important changes to the tale and in the 1857 edition of *Children's & Household Tales* included a line spoken by the huntsman when he encounters the engorged wolf sleeping in Granny's bed: 'So, I've found you at last, you old sinner. I've been looking for you a long time.' This edition also includes the suggestive line, 'After the wolf had satisfied his desires.' The words 'sinner' and 'desires' have many obvious connotations, particularly within the context of this tale, and their use strongly suggests that the wolf was known to the huntsman as a *sexual* predator.

The Brothers Grimm version of the tale conveys the girl's understanding that she must learn from her encounter with the wolf and use the experience to learn valuable life lessons, prompting her to promise herself to never again stray from the path. Bettelheim points out that in Perrault's tale no one actually warns Red Riding Hood not to dally on her way to her Grandmother's, or not to stray from the path. In the Grimm's version of the tale Red Riding Hood's mother is aware of her daughter's inquisitive nature and she warns the girl to stay on the path and not to 'peek into the corners' of Granny's house. While she exhibits an enquiring nature, the girl in the Grimms' story is also quite perceptive. When she arrives at Granny's house after her encounter with the wolf she notes a feeling of dread and uneasiness: 'It seemed so strange inside that she thought "Oh, my god, how frightened I feel today, and usually I like to be at Grandmother's".' Bettelheim suggests that the girl's intuition is rooted in an emotional response and her questions, which all relate to physical senses (hearing, seeing, touching and tasting), are her attempts to understand and comprehend the world. Of course, Carter's Red Riding Hood refuses these lessons in morality, choosing to liberate herself in her dead Granny's bed *between the paws of the tender wolf.*[32]

The versions of Red Riding Hood by Perrault and the Brothers Grimm were reprinted thousands of times in many different versions. They even became amalgamated with other oral and written variants to create yet more reinterpretations with many different meanings; a true testament to the malleability of the original tales and their continued relevance and ability to be retold, re read and reinterpreted. New versions specifically written for children became sanitised so the wolf rarely succeeded in devouring the grandmother or the girl. Countless literary revisions later and 'the nature of sexuality and gender stereotypes have been questioned and debated'[33] repeatedly with new variations reflecting changes in social attitudes and values.

RED HOODS, SILVER SCREENS

With its feisty heroine, formidable monster, rite-of-passage narrative and instantly familiar iconography, not to mention its dark undercurrents of violence, rape and bestiality, the tale of the young red-hooded woman and her lupine adversary has proved an irresistible source of inspiration for authors, artists and film-makers throughout the years.

Matthew Bright's cult indie classic *Freeway* (1996) updated the tale to feature Red Riding Hood (Reese Witherspoon) as a juvenile delinquent who attempts to track down her grandmother after her white-trash, drug-addicted parents are hauled off to prison. En route to her grandmother's she has a deeply disturbing encounter with Dr. Wolverton (Kiefer Sutherland), a deranged, paedophilic serial-killer masquerading as a child psychiatrist. Unfolding as a wickedly off-kilter road movie, *Freeway* also provides damning social commentary on the American justice system and its mistreatment of the young caught up within it, and not only speaks of the importance of friendship, loyalty and respect between young women, but the empowerment such kinship can ultimately bring about.

Directed by and starring David Morwick, *Little Erin Merryweather* (2003) updates the tale to feature Red Riding Hood as a serial killer with severe psychological issues which stem from abuse inflicted upon her by her father. A fairy tale-obsessed librarian, Erin (Vigdis Anholt) works on a university campus and preys on male students, stalking them through nearby woods, stabbing them to death and sewing up stones inside their bellies. Boasting the tag line 'A flash of red... Then you're dead', Morwick's film playfully warps gender conventions with its depiction of a female serial killer preying on a group of hapless young men.

Hard Candy (2005) featured Red Riding Hood (Ellen Page) as a teenaged vigilante using the internet to track down sexual predators and inflict her own brand of brutal justice upon them. Promotional artwork featured Page in a red hoodie standing in the jaws of a steel trap. Giacomo Cimini's *Red Riding Hood* (2003) similarly re-imagined the tale to tell of the misadventures of a young female vigilante delivering violent justice to thieves, rapists, murderers and thugs with the aid of her imaginary wolf mask-wearing friend, George. Harry Spark's ultra low-budget slasher *Rotkäppchen: The Blood of Red Riding*

Hood (2009) mixed erotic stylisation with gory violence in its story of a vicious serial killer preying on women, while the Syfy-commissioned *Red: Werewolf Hunter* (2010) put a sly spin on the tale as it followed the exploits of a modern-day descendant of Red Riding Hood. When Red (Felicia Day) brings her fiancé home to meet her family, a hardened clan of werewolf-hunters, trouble ensues when her beau is attacked by a werewolf and the pair must go on the run. She tries to protect him from her family while he attempts to suppress certain newly acquired animalistic urges.

A wonderfully subversive segment in Michael Dougherty's *Trick'r'Treat* (2007) features a group of teenaged girls partaking in a strange rite-of-passage initiation on All Hallows Eve. Gathering in the woods dressed as various Disney fairy tale heroines, it appears Laurie (Anna Paquin) and her friends will fall victim to a masked vampiric fiend. The girls finally reveal their true natures, though: they're a group of werewolves who relish hunting and devouring young men. It's telling that Laurie is dressed as Red Riding Hood and their ritual marks her entrance into adulthood. Proceedings are entrenched in the indulgence of the flesh, as the women copulate with and then slaughter the young men they've lured into the forest. Their conversations initially seem to be about Laurie losing her virginity and wanting to make her 'first time' special. By the conclusion of the segment, however, we come to know that her 'first time' does not refer to sex, but slaughter. The segment briefly skirts the same territory as *The Company of Wolves* as the girls ultimately celebrate their primal instincts and embrace their bloody desires.

Written by David Leslie Johnson (who also wrote *Orphan* [2009], which exploits the fairy tale figure of the changeling to creepy effect) *Red Riding Hood* (2011) was directed by Catherine Hardwicke, whose films frequently tell of marginalised young women struggling to find their place in the world. With its supernaturally charged story boasting werewolves and angst-ridden teens embroiled in a quivering love triangle, *Red Riding Hood* featured a headstrong heroine (Amanda Seyfried), strikingly beautiful imagery and drew comparisons with Hardwicke's adaptation of teen vampire romance, *Twilight* (2008). While it would be easy to dismiss her as a peddler of pallid, Gothic-lite romances, Hardwicke also co-wrote and directed the hard-hitting wayward-teen drama *Thirteen* (2003), which also charted the coming of age of a young woman, but in a manner as far removed from *Twilight* as is possible.

The characters, motifs and iconography of Red Riding Hood have also manifested on the small screen in television series such as *Grimm* (2011-present), a supernatural cop drama in which a homicide detective (David Giuntoli) discovers he is descended from a long line of hunters who fight supernatural creatures known as Wesen. *Grimm* frequently features plots and characters inspired by Grimms' fairy tales and the pilot featured a wolf-man who preyed on women who wore red. *Once Upon A Time* (2011-present) tells of the residents of Storybrooke, Maine, who are all actually characters from various fairy tales transported to the 'real world' and robbed of their memories by an evil curse. The character of Ruby (Meghan Ory), a waitress who lives with her Grandmother, is revealed to be Red Riding Hood. She's also revealed to be a werewolf and the only thing that prevents her from changing into a ravenous beast is her red cloak, which she must wear during a full moon.

No stranger to literature, the figure of Red Riding Hood has strolled through the pages of works as exciting and diverse as Angela Carter's *The Bloody Chamber*, Tanith Lee's 'Wolfland' (1982) and 'Bloodmantle' (1989), Roald Dahl's *Revolting Rhymes* (1982), in which the girl 'whips a pistol from her knickers' to defend herself from the wolf, Andrea L. Peterson's web-comic *No Rest for the Wicked* (2003-2012), in which Red is 'often seen carrying an axe, but is rarely seen chopping any wood', Benkyo Tamaoki's manga comic *Tokyo Red Hood* (2003-2004) and Neil Gaiman's *The Sandman* (1989-present). As one of the most popular fairy tales in the world, Red Riding Hood will continue to be adapted, reinterpreted and undergo interesting and relevant changes, ensuring the girl and her story will never be forgotten or devoured by the big bad wolf.

FOOTNOTES

1. Zipes (2007) p28
2. *The Company of Wolves* Special Edition DVD Commentary
3. Bettelheim (1976) p182
4. Tatar (1999) p17
5. Bettelheim (1976) p168
6. Zipes (2000b) p744
7. De Blécourt (2015) p6
8. Cited in Zipes (2012) p58

9. Cited in Zipes (2012) p58
10. Zipes (2000a) p302
11. Bettelheim (1976) p172
12. Duncan (2013) p29
13. Bettelheim (1976) p176
14. Cited in Bettelheim (1976) p176
15. Zipes (2013) p156
16. Tatar (2003) p199
17. Zipes (2000a) p302
18. Zipes (2007) p30
19. De Blécourt (2015) pg 6
20. De Blécourt (2015) pg 7
21. Zipes (2012) p29
22. ibid.
23. Tatar (1999) p6
24. Tatar (1999) p7
25. Rockett & Rockett (2003) pg 43
26. ibid.
27. Carter (1995) p110
28. Rockett & Rockett (2003) pg 43
29. Rockett & Rockett (2003) pg 45
30. Bettelheim (1976) p178
31. Bettelheim (1976) p174
32. Carter (1995) p118
33. Zipes (2000a) p302

CHAPTER FOUR: SEEING RED

'The pleasure would come from knowing the power she had.'
Rosaleen, *The Company of Wolves*

At the heart of *The Company of Wolves* is a story of sexual awakening, transformation – both literal and figurative – and the empowerment of women. Like the short stories from *The Bloody Chamber* upon which it is based, it carries a strong feminist message. Feminism is not a singular concept. It has held many differing, highly disputed positions throughout the years; it is constantly evolving and has, as Easton suggests, an 'internally conflicted history'.[1] Carter strongly identified as feminist, noting, 'I would regard myself as a feminist writer, because I'm a feminist in everything else and one can't compartmentalise these things in one's life'.[2] Throughout her career, her writing was informed by feminist principles. She claimed: 'My life has been most significantly shaped by my gender […] I spent a good many years being told what I ought to think, and how I ought to behave, and how I ought to write, even, because I was a woman and men thought they had the right to tell me how to feel, but then I stopped listening to them and tried to figure it out for myself but they didn't stop talking, oh, dear no. So I started answering back.'[3]

Carter's brand of feminism represents one strand and it was often at odds with those of other feminists at the time; aspects of it were even considered highly controversial. Her interest in pornography as a form liberating for women was particularly criticised and her writing on prostitution was described as having 'more to do with the lofty dreams of the intellectual in her study than the struggles of working girls on the streets'.[4] Characterised by the time in which she wrote, her socialist values, the fact that she was a white, heterosexual, middle class Englishwoman, Carter was seen as atypical because she was concerned with understanding and exploring sexual relations and conflicts between men and women when sections of feminism during this time were more concerned with the exploration of relationships between women. While she could 'imagine women as flawed and imperfect, necessarily so given the misogynistic world in which they lived',[5] she also distanced herself from her peers because she chose backdrops of the fantastic and the Gothic to explore her ideas – a far cry from the realist approach popular at the time. Her attitude and approach is beautifully complemented by Jordan, whose similar predilection for deconstructing normative gender roles and sexuality is evidenced throughout his work.

Carter sought to expose how we perceive women's sexuality as a myth instigated and perpetuated by moral and social conditioning. Her heroines struggle out of 'the straitjackets of history and ideology and biological essentialism',[6] and their struggle usually begins with curiosity as well as a willingness to act upon it. While traditional fairy tales condemned curiosity, especially in women, and curious natures frequently led to punishment, in Carter's reinterpretations inactivity and passivity are never condoned. Throughout her career, Carter would frequently visit the world of fairy tales to critique culturally constructed notions relating to women, gender roles and femininity, and by using fairy stories such as Red Riding Hood Carter not only explored how the tales were used to enforce certain ideas regarding women's sexuality and how they policed sexuality generally, but how they could also *liberate* sexuality. She utilised the figures of Red Riding Hood and the werewolf to explore notions of women's sexuality and desire; by allowing her Red Riding Hood to reclaim her autonomy through the acknowledgement of her sexuality, Carter consistently challenged the way in which women were represented as passive victims. Of her interest in using the form of the fairy tale to expose and critique cultural constructions of gender roles, she once said, 'I am all for putting new wine in old bottles, especially if the pressure of the new wine makes the old bottles explode'.[7] Carter viewed fairy tales as the oral literature of the common people and maintained that even though these stories were shaped and repurposed by seventeenth- and eighteenth-century aristocratic writers who wrote them down to preserve them and use them as lessons in behaviour and morality, there was still no denying the 'darkness and the magic'[8] inherent in their original content. She asserted that the stories were 'vast repositories of outmoded lies, where you can check out what lies used to be a la mode and find the old lies on which new lies are based'.[9]

Commenting on the proactive nature of typical fairy story heroines, Carter posited that 'you could not – could you? – say that the Sleeping Beauty was "a figure full of get up and go"?' Carter believed the time had come for the power of these heroines to not only be reclaimed, but brandished.[10] She viewed Red Riding Hood – specifically Charles Perrault's version (see **Red Hoods, Dark Woods**), stamped as it was by his ideas of how young, upper class women should behave – as a tale told to make young women wary of their own sexuality. By returning to Red Riding Hood the autonomy and resourcefulness Perrault stripped from her, Carter transformed her heroine from a passive victim to an active protagonist. The wolves Rosaleen encounters when she wilfully strays from the path do not drag her to hell as her Granny threatened; they speak of the girl's sexuality and the power it can unleash when it is not denied.

Several feminist critics have argued that because Carter used the form of the fairy tale, described by some as an inherently reactionary form that inscribes 'a misogynistic ideology',[11] Carter locked herself into the conservative sexism she was attempting to confront and deconstruct. Andrea Dworkin, a radical feminist whose views were often at odds with more liberal feminists and whose staunch views on pornography clashed with those of Carter, contended fairy tales perpetuate gender stereotypes, stating, 'we never did have much of a chance [...] we (the girls) aspired to become that object of every necrophiliac's lust – the innocent, victimized Sleeping Beauty, beauteous lump of ultimate, sleeping good'.[12] However, Alison Lurie argues that fairy tales 'suggest a society in which women are as competent and active as men, at every age and in every class'.[13] She cites Gretel defeating the cannibalistic witch and notes that for every youngest son, there is a youngest daughter, equally resourceful – and as they're not only the youngest, but also female, these characters have most to prove. Lurie also reminds us that figures such as fairy godmothers, witches and cruel stepmothers occupy privileged positions of power and active agency. Carter's work demonstrates that the form of the fairy tale, and the sexist binary oppositions which frequently operate within it, is not fixed; it can change and evolve to reflect shifting social attitudes and values. *The Bloody Chamber* provides a critique of fairy tales as texts that have had an impact on people's perceptions and attitudes towards gender on a broadly cultural level, and throughout it Carter's approach is deconstructive and transformative. For Carter, it was 'a book of stories *about* fairy stories'.[14] While certain critics claimed her reinterpretations just consisted of obvious reversals of plot conventions by letting the girl obtain the upper hand, Carter did not simply rewrite these stories to feature active female protagonists; she purposely referenced the original stories and how they portrayed women – a connotative sentence here, the conjuring of a specific image there – within the new stories and she did so in such a way that it was possible to compare and contrast both texts. Most importantly though, Carter created subjective female characters and gave each of them their own distinct voices and stances. In doing so, she demonstrated a disparate and multi-hued representation of women's sexuality traditionally denied them by fairy tales and the culturally constructed ideas of womanhood those tales typically substantiate. Her stories demonstrate a mutual 'awe and fear in the beasts, as well as in the beauty, and the reversal theme reinforces the equality of the transactions'.[15] After the consummation of the mutual desire between Red Riding Hood and the Huntsman, he becomes a tender wolf. By doing this, Carter enabled the reader to comprehend how her stories not only uncannily echoed the old tales, but offered self-contained critiques of them and demonstrated how her heroines gained self-awareness and understanding of others by embracing what was denied them by dominant cultural structures. Indeed, Carter's boldly feminist critique of these fairy tales, explored in themes of power, sexuality and the patriarchal construction of gender roles, prompted one critic to suggest that Carter had 'declared war on the myths of western culture'.[16]

Some critics, such as Patricia Duncker, claim the tale of Red Riding Hood, and indeed *The Company of Wolves*, conveys a message that willing acceptance is the only way to survive male aggression. Duncker described *The Company of Wolves* as a masochistic rape parable in which 'Red Riding Hood sees that rape is inevitable […] and decides to strip off, lie back and enjoy it. She wants it really. They all do'.[17] According to Jordan, Carter's basic narrative point was that when Rosaleen meets the Huntsman, she's unafraid, and it's her lack of fear that protects her. In the short story 'The Company of Wolves', Red Riding Hood is more than able to fend for herself. When she comments on the size of the wolf's teeth and he retorts 'All the better to eat you with', she *burst out laughing; she knew she was nobody's meat* [Carter uses the motif of flesh to signify pleasure and meat as signifying objectification]. *She laughed at him full in the face, she ripped off his shirt for him and flung it in the fire, in the fiery wake of her own discarded clothing.*[18] This is *not* a girl to willingly accept male aggression. By reconceptualising the beasts of these fairy tales as aspects of the female resolve for autonomy and pleasure, and by constructing femininity as active, hungry and even unruly, Carter fully acknowledged that women can have the desire to be beastly. Rosaleen's choice to become a wolf and join her lupine suitor at the film's climax speaks of the power her sexuality offers when it is not denied. Rosaleen embraces this and in doing so, *The Company of Wolves* acknowledges that women are not just objects of desire, but desiring subjects.

While some critics suggested *The Company of Wolves* was unable to subvert the binary divide of victim and aggressor, Anwell claimed it highlighted the complexity of representations of sexuality in Carter's work: 'The story, with its subversion of the familiar and its structure of story-telling within a story, suggests an ambiguity and plurality of interpretations which reminds us of our own capacity to dream […] Not only does the material world shift its laws; we experience our own capacity for abnormal behaviour.'[19] Others such as Duncker however, suggested that Carter's stories in *The Bloody Chamber* portray men as beasts and women as nothing but victims of male violence. The beasts of Carter's stories are actually projections of the feminine libido and autonomous female desire; Carter is not just asserting female aggression but arguing for recognition of a wider spectrum of women's sexuality, to demonstrate that it can also exhibit a range of distortions and perversions alongside what is considered 'normal.' Throughout *The Company of Wolves*, parallels between wolves and female sexuality are established (see 'A She-Wolf Came…'); both are powerful and frequently misunderstood or misrepresented and even persecuted. While perhaps more traditionally associated with dominant male sexuality, the wolves in Rosaleen's dreams represent sexual appetite, danger and desire; something women are warned off from exploring or experiencing in fairy tales. As a cultural construction, women's sexuality is denied a complex, polymorphous nature since this wouldn't fit into a comfortable concept of the 'feminine'. Phallocentric constructions of female sexuality either completely deny it, forcing it into a state of non-existence by insisting upon purity and virginal demureness in women, or regard it as ravenous and transgressive – something which must be tethered and contained. As Rosaleen gradually realises that her sexual appetites are not as evil as her Granny insists, and turns away from the preconceptions the old woman has attempted to instil within her, Rosaleen saves herself and attains autonomy.

DIFFERENT WOMEN, DIFFERENT VOICES

Various critics have questioned whether Carter's feminist reinterpretations of fairy tales could be adapted for the screen without losing their core feminist message. While many have praised the film as a radical retelling of the stories and, as Crofts notes, a 'productive engagement between feminism and the mainstream',[20] others claim Carter's feminist message was diluted to make it more marketable for mainstream audiences. Anwell argues that the film's reliance on special effects to depict painful, violent werewolf transformations detracted from the feminist power of the original stories, and that they convey little of the source stories' troubling ambiguities about the *possibility* of violence. However, she doesn't take into consideration that violence is an inherent aspect of Carter's work and is rife throughout *The Bloody Chamber*. In the words of Merja Makinen, Carter's texts were known for 'the excessiveness of their violence and, latterly, the almost violent exuberance of their excess. Many a reader has found the savagery with which she can attack cultural stereotypes disturbing'.[21] Throughout her career Carter unflinchingly explored the physical and psychological abuse suffered by women in phallocentric cultures and she offered representations of 'women who grab their sexuality and fight back [...] women troubled by and even powered by their own violence'.[22] With her invocation of strong, feminine sexuality, Carter insists that women can choose to be beastly, violent and erotic; it is by empowering themselves they are able to make this choice in the first place. She actively annihilates the stereotype of the passive, reactive female.

Carter's use of violence, coupled with what she was saying about gender politics, prompted Jones to suggest that her status as a feminist was 'highly debatable [...] her transformations do come disturbingly close to rape fantasies, in which, overpowered and deflowered by beastly, phallic men, women themselves attain a kind of beastly transcendence'.[23] It's important to remember that Carter deliberately chose stories that were already violently sexual in their subject matter and that she reinterpreted them to draw out their latent subtexts. When critics such as Anwell and Jones cite the violence in Carter's tales as problematic, they are denying that women, as Carter strives to demonstrate, can themselves be aggressive or violent, particularly in sexual drive. To deny this is to deny the polymorphous nature of female sexuality and to consign women to former whitewashed stereotypes such as the virginal bride, the demure damsel in distress or the unsexual Victorian 'Angel in the house'.

By looking at the stories being told throughout the film, and by observing *who* is telling them and why, one can see how Carter and Jordan foreground its exploration of the unstable, brittle nature of culturally constructed gender roles. By imbuing Rosaleen with

a more active vocal role, *The Company of Wolves* offers not only greater articulation
of female subjectivity, but becomes a film about the diversity of women's voices and
the expansive range of gendered experiences. When Anwell suggested the violent
transformations stripped the story of its female subjectivity, she commented that, 'the
blood and violence of the transformations are linked to sexuality in a way that recalls
the standard horror movie, in which the girl is seen as victim'.[24] The four stories in the
film are told by women and Anwell fails to note how the voices of these women are
used as signifiers of subjectivity. Rosaleen's tales feature women occupying positions
of power, knowledge and experience; and in Granny's tales, men are depicted as
aggressors and described as beasts. Granny's morally conservative agenda is to frighten
and indoctrinate Rosaleen through stories provoking anxiety, promising punishment
for deviation and rendering women as victims. Granny's stories reinforce conventional
gender roles as dictated by patriarchal oppression and reinforce ideas of aggressive male
sexuality.

There are also subtle differences in the depictions and contexts of the transformations
in each story. The first transformation occurs in Granny's story of a woman who
unwittingly marries a werewolf. She is beaten by her second husband when her long-
thought-dead werewolf bridegroom reappears accusing her of adultery. When Rosaleen
remarks, 'I'd never let a man strike me', the old woman insists Rosaleen should avoid
men because 'they're as nice as pie until they've had their way with you. But once
the bloom is gone, the beast comes out'. It is not only this context Anwell failed to
appreciate when she said the violence of the film stripped away female subjectivity, but
the ambiguity of the actual werewolf in the story. Far from representing unleashed male
aggression and sexuality, it is a strangely pitiful victim as much as it is an aggressor. The
pain of the transformation and the mixture of terror, awe and sympathy of the wife's
expression as she watches it suggests something other than fear. Her first husband
tears off his own skin and births the animal within. According to Crofts, the wife at once
inhabits a space that renders her 'masochistic viewer and sadistic voyeur'.[25] The werewolf
may pose a threat of violence for the woman in this story, but the actual violence
inflicted upon her is dealt by her current husband, who beats her because of her
attraction to and sympathy for her first husband. The second husband is reinforcing his
dominance and punishing his wife for her sexuality as it threatens his masculinity; to think

she was sexual with anyone else is unacceptable to him. Rosaleen's response to the story links the violence in it to domestic violence, violence within marriage. Later, when Rosaleen awakens in the night and glimpses her parents having sex, she asks her mother, 'Does he hurt you? Does Daddy hurt you when he…' The girl's mother reassures her that 'If there's a beast in men, it meets its match in women, too'. In doing so she offers her daughter a different perspective from that of her Grandmother and lets her see that she has options; a way out, if she chooses to accept it, of the rigid social constructions perpetuated by Granny and her generation. When Rosaleen reflects 'sounds like the beasts Granny talked about', her mother warns her not to pay too much attention to the old woman, again enabling Rosaleen to see things from a different perspective.

Screaming in the mirror

Granny's next story, which tells of a boy who transforms into a werewolf when he meets the Devil in the forest, also emphasises aggressive and monstrous male sexuality, even going as far as likening it to pure evil. The story is brief but significant because Rosaleen actually identifies with the adolescent boy in it. After he has applied the ointment given to him by the Devil, the boy watches with increasing horror as he begins to sprout hair on his chest. At this point the camera pulls back from his screaming, grotesquely contorted face which is revealed to be framed in the dreaming Rosaleen's bedroom mirror. Back in the reality of the framing story, Rosaleen awakens suddenly and when she turns to the mirror, she doesn't see her own face, but the face of the

Feminine wisdom – Rosaleen shares a secret with her mother

screaming boy. She identifies with him and his plight as much as she fears him, prompting her to say, 'That's a horrid story, I didn't like it at all.'

When Rosaleen begins to tell her own stories, the transformations that occur in them are not graphic, and the women who appear in her stories hold positions of power and experience. These stories grant us access to Rosaleen's subjectivity as they articulate her desires, and when she tells her own stories she becomes an active agent. When Rosaleen waits for her father to return from hunting the wolf, she and her mother discuss the forthcoming winter and the wolves it will bring. Rosaleen pities the hunted wolf and, wondering what will happen to this 'beautiful creature she has dreams about',[26] repeats what her Granny said about wolves not being what they seem. When her mother asks how a wolf could be worse than it is, the girl replies 'Not worse, but *different*. Maybe it's not the wolf's fault.' She then tells her mother a story about a wedding party turned into wolves by a woman who was wronged by the groom, and how the woman cursed the wolves to come and serenade her every night. When her mother asks where she heard a story like that and what possible pleasure there could be gained from 'listening to a lot of wolves? Don't we have to do it all the time?' Rosaleen replies, 'The pleasure would come... from knowing the power she had...' The contrast between the witch's reaction to the transformations and that of the wife in

Granny's story – who represents the old woman's perception of women; timid and abused by men – is very clear. Far from being fearful, she throws back her head and laughs defiantly. She is not accepting of the groom's betrayal, she is the experienced and sexually assured heroine critics like Anwell claimed did not translate to the screen adaptation. The comical execution of this scene suggests Rosaleen is also trying to counter the fear her Granny instilled within her by telling such a strangely humorous story. Indeed, Fenton's score – a merry, calliope-inspired circus waltz – further highlights the absurd nature of the scene.

Later, when Rosaleen confronts the Huntsman in Granny's cottage, his transformation is highly feminised. With its strange imagery, it not only evokes childbirth as the inner wolf is birthed from his mouth, but, as Pramaggiore suggests, a reversal of conventional sexual imagery; the phallic muzzle of the wolf emerging out of, instead of penetrating, a vaginal orifice. The story Rosaleen tells the wounded wolf not only contradicts what Granny said about priests, but foreshadows Rosaleen's own transformation. The injured wolf-girl in her tale is a beautiful, harmless creature – a stark contrast to the aggressive, monstrous male werewolves of Granny's tales. When the wolf-girl is shot and wounded, she is helped by a priest who tends to her wounds and whispers comforting words of compassion to her. This moment reveals Rosaleen attempting to reconcile the worlds of animal and human, and, according to Crofts, it also marks a reconciliation 'between the sexes and repudiation of the psychology of male aggressivity and female victimhood promoted by granny'.[27] The threatening force in this story emanates from the fear and ignorance of the villagers who see the wolf as a threat and are too quick to shoot her.

While the witch and the she-wolf who appear in Rosaleen's stories are seemingly marginalised and relegated to the peripheries (the treetops, an underworld accessed through the village well) they still hold autonomy, experience and self-awareness, and do so from vantage points that elevate them above and beyond repressive cultural conditioning. They are products of Rosaleen's subjectivity and speak of her attempts to attain self-understanding and work out conflicting feelings brought about by her Granny's oppressive moralising.

Certain critics have argued Carter's feminist message, and the subjectivity she imbues her female characters with, is further diluted because the film is bound within the

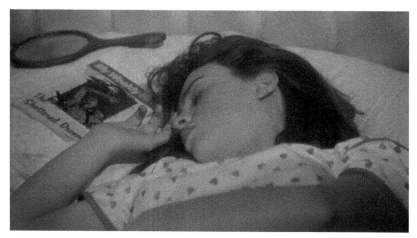

The shattered dream

confines of cinema's assumed dominant and sadistic masculine gaze. Feminist film theorist Laura Mulvey asserts 'the gaze' – what the camera shows us – objectifies women because it is configured as conveying an assumed (dominant) male spectatorial perspective. As such, it encourages gendered voyeurism in favour of an assumed male viewer through specific camera movements and narrative techniques that are traditionally aligned with the *male* spectator. Certain critics have suggested the film's framing device of the dreaming girl invites voyeurism and objectification because she is seemingly presented as an object to gaze at, and not depicted as a subject for the audience to identify with. Others, such as Crofts, counter this by arguing that *The Company of Wolves* shifts from the paradigm of the male gaze to the active female voice – such as when Rosaleen questions her Granny and begins to tell her own stories – by shifting the emphasis from the floating unspecified cinematic gaze to myriad women's voices and their use as signifiers of subjectivity and activity – therefore enabling a strong feminist reading which is further enhanced because of the different voices and the differing opinions and stances they express. This makes sense given the film's origins in literature and radio – where the voice would have been more appropriate to articulate subjectivity and convey a sense of identification, all the while foregrounding the importance of oral storytelling and the tales these works evolved from. The film's narrative also exists inside the dreaming girl's imagination and therefore, in the words of Crofts, offers an 'unusually strong point of insertion for the female spectator and foregrounding the subjectivity of the central protagonist and her developing awareness of her own sexuality'.[28] Indeed, the access we are granted to female subjectivity is reinforced when we cut to the reality of the framing story in the bedroom of the dreaming Rosaleen at various moments throughout and are reminded that what we see is unfolding within the dreams of a young girl.

THE LANGUAGE OF IMAGES

The playfulness of The Company of Wolves is typical of the work of both Jordan and Carter, both of whom have a postmodern approach to writing which not only toys with ideas of boundaries, gender, perception and identity, but does so through an enchanted mirror of references to other works and texts. It brims with signs, symbols and signifiers, and images and objects are laden with meaning. The Company of Wolves is not a probing character study; it is deeply metaphorical, its message conveyed through visual allegory and symbolism within stories within dreams. This symbolism is perhaps most evident in the scene where Rosaleen hides from the clumsy advances of the amorous village boy and climbs high into a tree from which various appendages suggestively protrude. This moment not only affords her, and the audience, the first glimpse of sky above the impenetrable forest, but aligns her with the witch who turned the wedding party into wolves, and who was also last seen in a treetop nursing her baby. In obtaining this new vantage point, both literal and figurative, Rosaleen's sexual maturation is effectively conveyed. In the treetop, she discovers a large nest belonging to a stork – a bird associated with fertility and the delivery of babies. Upon investigating the contents of the nest, she finds 'socially and biologically determined aspects of femininity';[29] eggs, a mirror and lipstick, each laden with their own symbolic meaning. Pondering her own reflection in the little handheld mirror, Rosaleen applies the red lipstick and, while admiring her image, notices the little eggs begin to crack and open, as though signifying her passage into womanhood and sexual potential.

This moment echoes certain ideas concerning self-awareness and identification explored in 'Wolf-Alice'. The significance of the mirror alludes to Lewis Carroll's Alice Through the Looking Glass and the psychoanalytical works of Jacques Lacan – whose

Investigating the nest

One last look

Mirror in the snow

work Carter frequently alluded to in her own writing – specifically his writings on the 'stade du miroir' (mirror state) which is based on the idea that when infants recognise themselves in a mirror they experience apperception; the objectification of one's self, and the ability to view one's self from outside one's self. It is interesting to note that when she meets the Huntsman later, Rosaleen abandons her mirror, and with it her socially determined femininity, letting the fast-falling snow cover it. No longer *an unbroken egg*,[30] Rosaleen stands at the threshold of adulthood, and, casting aside the idea of virginity as a prerequisite of redemption her Granny tried to instil within her, prepares herself to discard it, like her red cloak, when it is no longer needed. Rosaleen is neither the willing rape victim that Dunckner suggests she is, nor the 'fallen woman' Bettelheim described Red Riding Hood as – she is a young woman becoming confident in her own sexuality and her own desire for sexual experience; 'neither Justine, martyred by passive acceptance of her fate, nor Juliet, equating sexuality with violence'.[31] When she encounters the Huntsman, she is immediately curious and they share a mutual if initially hesitant pleasure in each other's company. Her blood-red shawl is a sexual symbol linked with puberty, menstruation and the loss of virginity with the breaking of the hymen; it is now discarded and thrown on the fire, as she figuratively discards her role as child, and as the victim her Granny would cast her as.

Another criticism aimed at the film concerns its climax, when the dreaming Rosaleen awakens in the framing narrative and screams in apparent terror, and the climax within the dream itself, when Rosaleen confronts the Huntsman in Granny's cottage. Concerning the latter, Anwell notes that Rosaleen not only shoots the Huntsman in desperation, but in the following moments in which she comforts the wounded wolf, the film is effectively robbed of Carter's victorious heroine sleeping '*between the paws of the tender wolf*'. She claims that Jordan presents a 'well worn image of Victorian sentimentality involving animals and children'[32] and that Rosaleen's off-screen transformation denies the viewer 'an image of successful sexual initiation';[33] this is proclaimed to be a compromise to mainstream audiences because it restricts 'the expression of sexuality and the girl's metamorphosis into a she-wolf'.[34] We don't need to see Rosaleen transform, though. Throughout the film, as she oscillates between childhood and adulthood, Rosaleen's ambivalence is organically connected with the figure of the werewolf. Her sympathy for the wolves, her questioning of Granny's conservative warnings, her sexual maturation, adolescent bodily changes and the stories she tells all link her inextricably to the figure of the werewolf. As Jones noted, 'for Carter, the transformation from human to wolf governed by the cycle of the moon, is connected to the menstrual cycle, also lunar',[35] thus suggesting Rosaleen's transformation into a wolf is inevitable. As noted elsewhere, the transformations throughout the film challenge traditional notions of gender and identity; the male werewolves are feminised through their transformations, and Rosaleen's subsequent unseen transformation is unleashed, along with her desire, in a moment of extreme ambiguity when the 'sex, gender and species of the transitioning werewolf are indeterminate'.[36] Furthermore, by refusing to depict her transformation the film closely links the metamorphosis of Rosaleen – and indeed the wolf-girl – to the transitions described in Carter's short stories, which were not graphic but subtly suggested. This approach further highlights differences in Granny's werewolf stories, with their hideous descriptions of brutal transformation, from Rosaleen's stories, in which transformations are weirdly comic or in the case of the wolf-girl, occur quietly and peacefully.

This ambiguity seeps into the dreaming Rosaleen's waking world during the film's climax and counters criticism of Jordan's surrender to mainstream appeal. While some critics have suggested the end of the film corrupts the empowering feminist message when Rosaleen wakes up and screams as the wolves of her dreams prowl into her bedroom, Jordan's unwillingness to provide a neatly resolved conclusion makes sense given his interest in exploring the boundaries between dream and reality and the ever-shifting relationship between them. The ambiguity established within her dreams has emerged into Rosaleen's waking world, which has become markedly different from how it seemed earlier; it has fallen into a state of disrepair, with vines and foliage consuming the furniture and walls of her house. While her actions in her dreams were empowering, upon waking, is she once again relegated to the role of victim in a world that has constructed her as such because of her gender? Has she relinquished control of her transition into adulthood? Did she ever have control of it? Her family are nowhere to be seen and she finds herself, once again, in a strange twilight place hovering between worlds and states of mind. If the horror offered by *The Company of Wolves* speaks of the disintegration of boundaries between what is internalised and externalised, Jordan's denouement leaves Rosaleen suspended in an uncanny, 'somewhere-in-between' place where she is neither awake nor asleep, and in the words of Pramaggiore, a space that 'lacks the categories of girl/woman, human/monster, self/other, or reality/representation'.[37] It is also important to note that when Rosaleen awakens and screams, it is after she has told her own story of the wolf-girl. The casting of Danielle Dax as the wolf-girl is highly significant. Through her status as a cult underground music icon, Dax represents a very specific kind of punk feminist ethos and she embodies an alternative representation of womanhood, one not tethered to patriarchal construction. Dax's unique vocal style, alongside women like Diamanda Galas, Lydia Lunch, Tori Amos and P.J. Harvey, renders the scream less an act of terror and submission than a rejection of normative artistry and a reconnection with primal instincts. It becomes a primal mode of expression that is being embraced and returned to, a means to construct one's own identity and representation as a speaking subject.

MAIDENS AND MONSTERS

The Company of Wolves belongs to a group of films which unravel as darkly sexual coming of age parables, with fantastical narratives in which adolescent girls on the cusp of adulthood find themselves in menacing, arguably psychological landscapes pursued by literal and figurative monsters they conjure and encounter therein. With their dreaming girl protagonists, whose waking and dream worlds become suffused to the point of saturation, titles such as The Wizard of Oz (1939) and The Curse of the Cat People (1944) can be regarded as significant cinematic precursors of The Company of Wolves. Indeed, The Curse of the Cat People was described as a moody fantasy that 'emerges as an oddly touching study of the working of a sensitive child's mind'.[38] The transformation that occurs when young girls pass from childhood into adulthood is also the main concern of Lucile Hadžihalilović's Innocence (2004) and several notable titles by French film-maker Catherine Breillat, including A Real Young Girl (1976), Bluebeard (2009) and Sleeping Beauty (2010). Like The Company of Wolves these films explore adolescent sexuality from the perspective of young women and often incorporate elements of fantasy and the Gothic into dream-like narratives. Titles such as Valerie and Her Week of Wonders (see **Once Upon A Time**), Lemora – A Child's Tale of the Supernatural (1973), Labyrinth (1986), Return to Oz (1985), Paperhouse (1988), Celia: Child of Terror (1989) and Pan's Labyrinth (2006) explore and unfold within the dreams and waking-fantasies of adolescent girls, who must use their resourcefulness, strength and virtue to overcome danger and emerge into adulthood victorious and transformed. These films are all about choice, and while their young protagonists seek comfort and escape from hardships and tensions in worlds of their own creation, none wait passively to be saved. They all choose to be active, defiant and to attain control. The narratives through which these girls wander echo the initiations of folk and fairy tales in which the girl must outsmart the monster to obtain knowledge and experience.

Historically, it is rare for women to be portrayed as the questing, proactive heart of non-genre movies. Myriad fantasy films of course feature young male protagonists, but by comparison adolescent female protagonists tend to appear in 'more adult, offbeat fantasy films, weaving a complex emotional path through the narrative and exerting a much darker, stranger and more powerful pull than Harry Potter could ever muster'.[39] One of the reasons these female adolescents are so compelling is that the thrust of the drama hinges on their perceived vulnerability. If femininity is constructed as weak and passive by patriarchal society, and the young are considered equally weak and in need of protection, it's not unreasonable to conclude that an adolescent girl is a figure representing ultimate vulnerability. The dramatic effect of the perils encountered by these characters is emphasised by their status as young women, and this grants them an outsider's perspective from which to view the world and counterpoint their vulnerability. Like Rosaleen, however, these young women prove themselves to be anything but vulnerable; they are by turns resourceful, inquisitive, headstrong, authentic and full of conviction.

When women film-makers experiment with the fairy tale to talk about women's sexuality and gendered experience, the stories they tell of adolescent girls getting lost so they can emerge transformed into the world are, in the words of Guillermo del Toro, 'typically […] intelligent, complex and empowering'.[40] One such film-maker is Catherine Breillat, whose uncompromising and frequently controversial body of work focuses almost exclusively on female sexuality – particularly female adolescent sexual awakening – gender conflict and sibling rivalry. A Real Young Girl (which is based on her own novel, Le Soupirail [1974]), 36 Fillette (1988) and À ma sœur! (2001) form a thematic trilogy and boast narratives filtered solely through the perspectives of their sullen, sexually curious adolescent girl protagonists. Throughout their respective narratives these girls invasively contemplate and explore their developing bodies, enter complex relationships with older men and regard their virginity as an obstacle to overcome on the way to adulthood. They are all confused and awed by their changing bodies and are as terrified and repulsed by their burgeoning sexuality as they are eventually empowered by it. Breillat's work has frequently been labelled pornographic (*A Real Young Girl* provoked so much controversy upon its release it was banned outright for years) and often her characters exist as mouthpieces through which she articulates her own philosophies regarding gender roles and women's sexual desire. While these titles differ from *The Company of Wolves* in their unsentimental and highly explicit approach to the core subject matter, they feature characters who, like Rosaleen, resist the confinement imposed upon their gender by patriarchal society. Some of them also inhabit sensual dreamscapes which gradually encroach or violently interject upon their waking worlds. These titles also share Carter's unwavering acknowledgment of the polymorphous nature of women's sexuality – encompassing everything from fragile to fearsome – and feature characters who reject patriarchal forms of social and self-regulation.

More recently Breillat has turned to the fairy tale to broaden her exploration of gender conflict and women's sexuality. *Bluebeard* and *Sleeping Beauty* bear a much stronger kinship, both tonally and spiritually, with *The Company of Wolves*. Like the tales concerning Pandora and her box, the fate of Lot's wife and Cupid's seduction of Psyche, Charles Perrault's literary fairy tale 'Bluebeard' is chiefly concerned with the punishment of curious women. Breillat's subversive feminist adaptation opens with a framing narrative featuring two young sisters who are reading the eponymous fairy story, which tells of Marie-Catherine (Lola Créton), a girl forced into marriage to save her fatherless, penniless family from destitution. Her husband is Lord Bluebeard (Dominique Thomas), a formidable aristocrat whose previous wives all vanished without trace. Doting on his young wife, he gives Marie-Catherine keys to every door in the castle, all but one of which he invites her to open and explore the rooms beyond. During one of Bluebeard's many trips away, Marie-Catherine is overcome with curiosity and peeps inside the forbidden chamber, only to discover the bloodied bodies of her husband's previous wives. Upon his return, Bluebeard discovers his wife's indiscretion but before he can kill her as he did his previous wives, the wily Marie-Catherine turns the tables on her monstrous spouse and saves herself. Throughout the film Breillat offers barbed commentary on a society that would render women subservient and reliant on men for financial stability. The two sisters in the framing story frequently interrupt the main narrative to comment and reflect on various social attitudes towards gender roles.

With her second fairy tale adaptation Breillat completely upends the traditional depiction of Sleeping Beauty as a passive, inactive figure devoid of drive and will. Her princess is not at the mercy of external forces and when she falls into her bewitched 100-year slumber, she rushes headlong into an adventure entirely of her own making. Like Jordan's film, the narrative of Breillat's *Sleeping Beauty* unfolds within the dream-space of a slumbering girl, and in doing so it centres her in an active positon within the story. Princess Anastasia (Carla Besnaïnou) is a girl who prefers climbing trees and sword-fighting than performing in ballets. In her dream-state she sets off on a quest during which she encounters and defeats an ogre, loses a friend to the chilly allure of the Snow Queen, teams up with a feisty Romani girl bandit and befriends a pallid monarch. When Anastasia awakens a century later she is a young woman (Julia Artamonov) very much aware of her maturing sexuality. She encounters the great-grandson of her friend borne away by the Snow Queen, and her Romani friend also reappears all grown up to induct Anastasia into the heady realms of physical love. Throughout *Sleeping Beauty* Breillat conjures a world like the one Rosaleen inhabits where children yearn for adulthood but feel threatened by it and unsure of their place within it. Her reflections on gender roles and the ambivalence of adolescent desire speak of the cultural confinement of women. Like *The Company of Wolves*, *Sleeping Beauty* asserts that confinement can be escaped if young women embrace and explore their curiosity to emerge fully formed into adulthood.

Written and directed by Ann Turner, *Celia: Child of Terror* is another coming of age tale told from the perspective of its young protagonist. Set against the backdrop of 1950s suburban Australia, Turner's film tells of Celia (Rebecca Smart), a lonely girl grieving for her dead grandmother and trying to make sense of her father's infidelity. When it is discovered her new neighbours are members of the communist party, Celia's father (Nichols Eadie) becomes hostile to them and forbids his daughter to play with them. A government sanction to eradicate a rabbit population breeding dangerously out of control drives another wedge between Celia and her family when her pet rabbit is confiscated. Deprived of friends and her beloved pet, Celia blames her father and makes up a voodoo-esque ritual with masks and totemic objects to exact revenge. As she becomes unable to separate her imaginary world from the real world, a sudden act of violence corrupts her into premature adulthood. Like Rosaleen, Celia's reveries of folkloric beasts form her attempts to understand the complexities of adult behaviour.

Based upon the novel *Mine-Haha, or On the Bodily Education of Young Girls* (1903) by Frank Wedekind, Lucile Hadžihalilović's *Innocence* is a haunting and quietly sinister coming of age parable that allegorises female adolescence in a manner similar to Jordan's film. The story concerns a group of prepubescent girls living in a boarding school in the midst of a deep, dark forest. New pupils arrive in small coffins through a series of mysterious underground hallways and they are greeted and dressed by their peers. Different coloured ribbons are worn by the girls to mark different age groups – red for the youngest girls and violet for the older girls. The only adults at the school are two melancholy young women (Marion Cotillard and Hélène de Fougerolles) who teach the girls biology and ballet, and several serving staff; older women who are completely silent. During the night, the older girls must dance for a mysterious audience in a theatre reached by a door in an old grandfather clock. The butterfly wings they wear while performing not only represent their metamorphosis from girls to women, instigated by their sexual maturation, but also their entrapment – earlier one of the teachers shows the girls a series of butterflies she has pinned inside a glass box. When they begin to menstruate, the older girls are escorted from the school by the two teachers and the film's denouement suggests that the school was preparing the girls for their transition to womanhood, their transformation into sexual (and sexualised) women through a process of socialisation. Described as 'Buñuel meets Angela Carter meets Enid Blyton',[41] *Innocence* unfolds within a female-centric world as hermetically sealed as a dream, and is rife with uterine imagery of rushing water and long, dark subterranean passageways. The mysterious forest in which the boarding school nestles is 'of the sort usually inhabited by hungry wolves and little wayfarers in symbolic red hoods'.[42] Hadžihalilović evokes an atmosphere of menace and surreal beauty and conjures a lyrical fairy tale in her exploration of the rites and rituals of female adolescence.

Reflecting on the sources he looked to for inspiration while making *Pan's Labyrinth*, Guillermo del Toro cited Angela Carter's 'acknowledgement of the complexity and the potency of the female psyche'[43] in his efforts to avoid reducing his girl protagonist to a mere role-playing figure. While certainly not as concerned with ideas of sexual awakening as *The Company of Wolves*, *Pan's Labyrinth* nonetheless shares its fairy tale influences and fascination with the internal world of a young girl. Del Toro's most personal movie is an anti-fascist coming of age fairy tale in which the real monsters are human. Brutality collides with innocence as 11-year-old Ophelia (Ivana Baquero) escapes into a world of fantastical creatures, daring quests and uterine imagery to escape the horrors of her life during the Spanish Civil War. Offering a child's eye perspective of monsters, the horrors Ophelia encounters are, like the dreaming Rosaleen's, entirely of her own making; it is she who is in control. Her monsters, like Carter's werewolves, are powerful and ambiguous, scary, strange and beautiful; they are externalisations of Ophelia's internal processes as she struggles to comprehend adulthood and all the contrasting qualities that make us human. Del Toro claimed the simplicity and brutality of fairy tales were a major influence and he viewed Ophelia as Red Riding Hood and her stepfather, the merciless Captain Vidal (Sergi López), as the big bad wolf.

Several years after *The Company of Wolves*, similar adolescent dreamscapes to those glimpsed in Jordan's film would be explored in Bernard Rose's *Paperhouse* (1988). Based on Catherine Storr's novel *Marianne Dreams*, it tells of Anna (Charlotte Burke), a sickly young girl who creates and explores a strangely forbidding fantasy world inspired by drawings in her sketchpad. Jim Henson would also venture along a similar, albeit much less obviously sexual path with *Labyrinth*, which tells of Sarah (Jennifer Connelly), a young girl who must venture through troubles unknown to a grotesque fairy tale land to rescue her stepbrother from a cruel Goblin King. Like the werewolves in Jordan's film, regarded with empathy and terror, Jareth (David Bowie), the antagonist of *Labyrinth*, is loathed yet secretly desired by Sarah. Henson claimed *Labyrinth* was the story of a person at the point of changing from a child to a woman and that, for him, 'times of transition are always magic. Twilight is a magic time and dawn is magic – the times during which it's not day and it's not night, but something in between. That is what the film is about'.[44] When Sarah strays completely off the path and into the depths of the labyrinth, her experiences there and the choices she makes speak of her transition from childhood to adulthood. Indeed, *Labyrinth* enters a weirdly Freudian realm when one catches a glimpse of the photographs of Sarah's absent mother, an actress named Linda Williams, on her dresser mirror and in various scrapbooks. Her mother is pictured with the actor (Bowie again) she left her family for. Sarah finds that she too is tempted to make the same choice and abandon her family for a fantastical romance. Her interactions with the Goblin King can be seen as her struggle to reconcile her romantic feelings for her mother's lover who she casts as a monster in her guilt-ridden mind.

Recent titles with young women in empowered roles, such as *The Hunger Games* (2012), *Divergent* (2014) and *Mad Max: Fury Road* (2015) are indebted to these earlier fantasy films featuring active and defiant young women whose quietly staunch desire to follow their hearts, entreats them to move off the path and to find their own way through the deep, dark woods.

FOOTNOTES

1. Easton (2000) p3
2. Cited in Gruss (2009) p3
3. Easton (2000) p2
4. (2006) *Angela Carter: Glam rock feminist:* http://www.independent.co.uk/arts-entertainment/books/features/angela-carter-glam-rock-feminist-6097243.html
5. ibid.
6. Simpson, Helen (2006) *Femme fatale: Angela Carter's The Bloody Chamber:* https://www.theguardian.com/books/2006/jun/24/classics.angelacarter
7. Cited in Crofts (2003) p21
8. Makinen (2000) p22
9. ibid.
10. Clapp, Susannah (2012) *Angela Carter: Inside the Bloody Chamber:* http://www.theartsdesk.com/books/angela-carter-inside-bloody-chamber
11. Makinen (2000) p23
12. Tatar (1999) xiii
13. ibid.
14. Makinen (2000) p23
15. Makinen (2000) p29
16. Easton (2000) p7
17. Makinen (2000) p31
18. Carter (1995) p118
19. Anwell (1994) p82
20. Crofts (2003) p110
21. Makinen (2000) p20
22. Makinen (2000) p21
23. Jones (2002) p174
24. Anwell (1994) p84

25. Crofts (2003) p119
26. *The Company of Wolves* Special Edition DVD Commentary
27. Crofts (2003) p124
28. Crofts (2003) p121
29. Crofts (2003) p122
30. Carter (1995) p114
31. Cited in Anwell (1994) p81
32. Anwell (1994) p81
33. ibid.
34. Anwell (1994) p83
35. Jones (2002) p174
36. Pramaggiore (2008) p33
37. Pramaggiore (2008) p31
38. Crowther, Bosley: Review of *The Curse of the Cat People* (1944) http://www.nytimes.com/movie/review?res=950CE0D8153DE13BBC4C53DFB566838F659EDE
39. Cochrane, Kira (2007) *The Girl Can Help It*: http://www.theguardian.com/film/2007/apr/27/2
40. Del Toro (2013b) pp108-109
41. This quote from a review by The Independent on Sunday appears on the cover of Artificial Eye's DVD release of the film
42. http://www.nytimes.com/2005/10/21/movies/young-girls-and-their-bodies-all-for-the-sake-of-art.html
43. Del Toro (2013b) pp108-109
44. Cochrane, Kira (2007) *The Girl Can Help It*: http://www.theguardian.com/film/2007/apr/27/2

CHAPTER FIVE: THE BIG BAD WOLF

'The lore of lycanthropy and the manifold legends of werewolves are one of the oldest things in the world […] and it would hardly seem logical, upon the face of it, that there should be no foundation in fact for such widely spread – aye, and widely believed – stories...' Gerald Biss, *The Door of the Unreal*

A werewolf, or lycanthrope, is a person who transforms into a wolf. Stories and myths regarding humans turning into wolves have fascinated and terrified us for millennia. These stories have endured because they continue to speak of an elementary aspect of the collective human consciousness: beneath the veneer of civility, all of us harbour aggressive, animalistic impulses. Common perception of the werewolf derives from its myriad representations in folklore, literature and, perhaps most significantly, cinema. Lycanthropy occurs in several ways and varies throughout history. According to folklore and antiquated literature, such as *The Book of Were-Wolves* (1865) by Sabine Baring-Gould and *Werwolves* (1912) by Elliott O'Donnell, it is invoked as the result of a curse, or through the practice of diabolical occult rituals. Excommunication from the church and tainted bloodlines were also believed to incur metamorphosis. The most widespread ideas of lycanthropy as the result of infection caused when an individual is bitten by a werewolf, and activated by lunar influence, are recent and originate from Hollywood cinema.

Jordan and Carter drew upon olden lore as much as they did literature and cinema; Granny's warnings of wolves who are 'hairy on the inside' stems from an old belief that the werewolf wore its pelt under its human skin and turned itself inside out when transforming. The tales Granny tells Rosaleen – of the werewolf bridegroom and the boy meeting the Devil in the woods – are rooted in ancient European legends. In *Werewolf Histories* (2015) historical anthropologist and witchcraft scholar Willem de Blécourt references antiquated tales from Estonia and Russia concerning women who, like the luckless bride in Granny's tale, unwittingly marry werewolves. De Blécourt cites 'The Werewolf Husband', which tells of a man who transforms into a wolf and devours his bride. When he transforms back into a man, he is identified as the culprit because the threads of her clothing are still stuck between his teeth. Granny's tale of the boy who transforms into a werewolf when he meets the Devil in the forest is rooted in old folktales and legends that claimed lycanthropy resulted from the enacting of dark rituals and pacts with the Devil. In European folklore werewolves, like witches, were strongly associated with the occult and werewolf 'outbreaks' and trials took place in parts of France, Latvia and Estonia, where tales of werewolves were particularly rife. In 1912 paranormal 'scholar' Elliott O'Donnell published *Werwolves*, a tome intended as an encyclopedic study of lycanthropic activity and first-hand accounts of the author's encounters with werewolves. According to O'Donnell, in cases when lycanthropy was not hereditary, it could still be attained through the performance of ancient rites and holding communion with dark forces in the forest. He claimed certain unguents, potions and ointments were used – like the contents of the little tincture given to the boy by the Devil in Granny's story. Amongst ingredients said to aid the transformation process were asafoetida, parsley, opium, hemlock, saffron, aloe and the fat of a slaughtered animal. Once applied to the body, wolfish transformation ensued. Rosaleen's tale regarding a wedding party turned into wolves by a witch also has links to archaic superstitions regarding werewolves and weddings. According to Barry Lopez, author of *Of Wolves and Men* (1978), there is an old Polish belief that a belt of human skin laid across the threshold of a house where a wedding is being held will transform all who step over it into wolves.

Winter solstice, the longest night of year, was associated with werewolf transformation in certain cultures and the significance of Christmas in werewolf lore is alluded to during Rosaleen's encounter with the Huntsman. After hearing wolves howling outside Granny's snowed-in cottage, she asks, 'Who has come to sing us carols?' Carter explicitly references the link between Christmas and the birth of the werewolf in *The Bloody Chamber*: *Midnight, and the clock strikes. It is Christmas Day, the werewolves' birthday, the door of the solstice still wide enough open to let them all slink through.*[1] When Granny and Rosaleen visit Alice's grave, Granny warns Rosaleen that illegitimate children fathered by priests, babies born feet-first (an old Slavic superstition) and anyone born on Christmas Day, will become werewolves. Some of these old European beliefs are central to the idea of lycanthropy in Guy Endore's novel *The Werewolf of Paris* (1933) and its filmic adaptation, *The Curse of the Werewolf* (1961).

Most cultures throughout the world have tales about werewolves: the lycanthropos of Greece, the Loup-garou of France, the Spanish hombre-lobo. A genuine belief in werewolves raged throughout Europe in the Middle Ages. In the fifteenth century, a council of theologians was established by the Holy Roman Emperor Sigismund to investigate an epidemic of lycanthropy. The Greek historian Herodotus described the Neuri tribe as shamanic magicians who had the power to transform into wolves. Pliny the Elder claimed the family of Antæus, a physician whose remedy for rabies contained the skull of a hanged man, held an annual lottery to select a family member to be transformed into a wolf. Chantal Bourgault du Coudray notes several speculations regarding the origins of a belief in werewolves, including the crimes perpetrated by sociopaths and the tribal practices of clans donning animal skins to strike fear into the hearts of their enemies.[2] In the later Middle Ages werewolf trials ran parallel with witchcraft trials throughout Europe; those accused of being werewolves were forcibly exiled and persecuted. In European folklore werewolves, like witches, were strongly associated with the occult.

At the heart of the concept of lycanthropy is an exploration of the carnal instincts of mankind. The figure of the werewolf is positioned between civilised human society and primal bestiality, it straddles the boundaries between nature and culture, serving as a stark reminder of our primitive past. According to Bourgault du Coudray, if humans indeed evolved from animals, then traces of our primal past 'might linger in hidden recesses of the modern psyche'.[3] Possessing a Cartesian duality between mind and body, the werewolf is a thoroughly modern monster, a psychoanalytical expression of the inner conflict between human intellect and base instinct. Throughout literature and cinema, the werewolf is often used as a metaphor to explore mankind's primal instincts laid bare; the transformation strips away civility – and notions of order – and re-establishes our connection with dormant aggressions and appetites long suppressed through centuries of civilisation. According to Duncan, the werewolf's condition is the human condition, 'wildly inflated, terrifyingly enlarged: a creature capable of love, empathy, humour, imagination, reason and moral sense [...] but compromised by the thudding insistence of the plainer ones: hunger, aggression, libido'.[4] The divided self of the werewolf dramatises this schism and exposes raw bestial impulses that, in Freudian terms, were suppressed through the process of civilisation. Relegated to the realm of the unconscious these dormant instincts are the 'beast within'. The werewolf is frequently depicted as a cursed and shunned individual, thought to have no control over his bestial urges or monthly moonlit transformations. Some of the earliest werewolf stories are found in the myths, legends and poetry of antiquity, and in many of these early literary accounts of lycanthropy, such as *The Epic of Gilgamesh* – an epic poem from ancient Mesopotamia (2100 BC) – the metamorphosis of man into wolf is the result of a curse. The first significant 'literary' werewolf, a magician named Moeris, appears in Virgil's *Eclogue VIII* (37 BC). Moeris uses botanical remedies to transform himself into a wolf and, according to Leslie A. Sconduto, he is the first werewolf with a duel personality: as a wolf he is described as passive, but as a magician there is a 'vortex of violence around him'.[5] Ovid's *Metamorphoses* (8 AD) includes the story of Lycaon, King of Arcadia, who served the gods a meal of human flesh in order to test the omniscience of Zeus. As punishment, Zeus turned Lycaon into a wolf to expose his decadent moral appetites. Petronius's *Satyricon* (55 AD) also features an account of a werewolf; a young soldier revealed to be responsible for attacking and devouring local livestock when he exhibits identical injuries to those inflicted upon the beast during an attack, a trope that resonates throughout later accounts of the werewolf in literature and cinema.

The presence of the werewolf was quite frequent in medieval literature. One of the most significant depictions appeared in a translation of Marie de France's Breton lai 'The Bisclavaret' towards the end of the twelfth century. 'The Bisclavaret' contains certain motifs and plot points that would appear in other werewolf tales of the time, and tells of a man transformed into a werewolf by a curse. When his wife discovers his secret, she elopes with her lover leaving her husband trapped in wolf form. The wolf soon earns the trust and protection of the king and is eventually able to take revenge on his unfaithful wife and her lover and become human again. Several other werewolf tales in medieval literature, such as 'Guillaume de Palerne', 'Arthur and Gorlagon' and the Breton lais 'Biclarel' and 'Melion' follow a similar plot structure. According to Brian J. Frost, the eventual demise of the medieval romance also brought about the decline of the presence of the werewolf in literature, and it wouldn't be fully revived until the nineteenth century, when it found an appropriate abode in the shadowy realms of Gothic fiction. Richard Thomson's short story 'The Severed Arm; or, The Wehr-Wolf of Limousin', which appeared in *Tales of an Antiquary* (1828), recalls the basic plots of various medieval Breton lais and utilises a specific motif that would later become a common trope of werewolf fiction. It tells of treachery, curses and a knight transformed into a wolf. During a violent encounter the wolf-knight's forepaw is cut off and transforms into the arm of a man. This motif was central to Carter's short story 'The Werewolf', and found its way into the script for *The Company of Wolves*; when Rosaleen's father returns home from hunting the wolf that has been prowling through the forest he produces a bundle of rags containing a human hand. He insists that when he cut it off it was a wolf's forepaw. It also appears in Howard Wandrei's 'The Hand of the O'Mecca' (1935) in which a man unwittingly marries a werewolf. His bride attacks him in wolf form and when he cuts off her paw, he watches in horror as it turns into a human hand.

The folkloric notion of lycanthropy resulting from fraternisations with the Devil and old beliefs that werewolves could change form by practising occult rituals also began to creep into literature. George W.M. Reynold's *Wagner the Wehr-Wolf*, a sprawling Gothic melodrama, utilised this idea and is especially significant because the werewolf was also the protagonist. Serialised between 1846 and 1847, *Wagner the Wehr-Wolf* tells of an ailing shepherd who makes a pact with the Devil. In return for subservience to the Prince of Darkness, the shepherd is granted eternal life, but must also become a wolf for one day every month for the rest of his life. Alexandre Dumas's fantasy-romance *The Wolf Leader* (1857) tells of an unassuming shoemaker who, in order to obtain revenge on a pitiless nobleman, makes a pact with a werewolf. As a result of the pact, he finds he can command the wolves of the forest, which he uses to extract bloody revenge. Gerald Biss's *The Door of the Unreal* (1919), an epistolary novel written as a series of diary entries, letters and newspaper clippings, documents the investigation of a series of gruesome murders on a lonely stretch of road in the English countryside. The savage killer is revealed to be a werewolf; an old German professor who dabbles in the occult and various sinister alchemies. With its fragmented narrative comprised of various accounts by characters involved in the investigation, Biss's novel was heavily inspired by *Dracula* (1897).

Towards the end of the nineteenth century authors began to introduce psychological elements to werewolf literature, and, in the case of Robert Louis Stevenson, to utilise motifs associated with werewolf fiction in order to explore ideas regarding psychology and identity. According to Peter Penzoldt, Stevenson's *Olalla* (1885) was 'the first story in literature in which a case of insanity is not only correctly described but is also correctly diagnosed' and he described it as 'the most convincing werewolf story there is'.[6] Stevenson would more famously use the werewolf motif again in *The Strange Case of Dr Jekyll and Mr Hyde* (1886). While not, strictly speaking, a werewolf story, it nonetheless contains strong thematic parallels in its investigation of one man's unleashed primal impulses and destructive, salacious cravings. Stevenson's allegory depicts the renowned Dr. Jekyll's struggle to reconcile disparate aspects of his own psyche when he creates a serum that separates his very personality, creating Mr Hyde, an alter-ego who lives out Jekyll's most suppressed and dangerous desires. The inner conflict experienced by the doctor speaks of the dual nature of mankind that nestles at the very core of the concept of lycanthropy. Written during a time when the idea of physiognomy was gaining popularity, the hideous nature of Dr. Jekyll's inner self is reflected in the outer appearance of the monstrous Mr. Hyde. Other psychological werewolf stories and the idea of 'lycanthropic madness' include 'The Man Wolf' (1860) by Emile Man and Alexandre Chatrian, which tells of a decrepit Count's cursed lineage and descent into lunatic ravings – he resembles a wolf in everything but form. Lycanthropic madness abounds throughout Arthur Conan Doyle's 'A Pastoral Horror' (1890), significant aspects of which would echo throughout Stephen King's *Cycle of the Werewolf* (1983), particularly in its revelation of the maniac's identity. Carter and Jordan would take a similar approach with *The Company of Wolves* as its werewolves are arguably psychological, appearing as they do in the dreams of an adolescent girl, and are used metaphorically to address ideas concerning the emergence of adult sexuality.

Like Biss's *The Door of the Unreal*, Guy Endore's *The Werewolf of Paris* (1933) also took inspiration from Stoker's classic novel. It is loosely based on a bloodthirsty historical figure, Sergeant Francois Bertrand, a French solider whose diabolical deeds were alleged to include exhuming the bodies of the recently deceased to feast upon their flesh. Adapted for the screen as *The Curse of the Werewolf*, Endore's novel tells of Bertrand Caillet, the eponymous beast whose monthly transformations are the result of a tainted heritage. Conceived when a ghoulish priest rapes his young mother, and born on Christmas Day (when an unwanted child was regarded as an insult to Heaven because of its subversion of the holy implications of the birth of Christ), Caillet is marked as 'different' from birth, with his hairy palms, eyebrows that meet in the middle and a proclivity for howling in the night. According to Frost, Endore's novel was significant because it was the first to link the figure of the werewolf with sexuality. Caillet's transformations begin when he enters adolescence (see '**A She-Wolf Came…**') coinciding with the sexual urges he experiences. The increasingly sadomasochistic relationship between Caillet and his mistress Sophie stresses the psychosexual aspect of lycanthropy, something which few stories did prior. Endore's novel echoes the sentiments of certain mid-nineteenth century French and English Decadents, including the poet and critic Charles Baudelaire, who suggested the sadistic elements of human sexuality were ideally represented by the figure of the werewolf; pain coupled with sexual pleasure and an unconscious desire to 'devour' a lover.[7] This aspect of Endore's work strongly influenced Carter as she also used the figure of the werewolf to address notions of sexuality and lust in *The Company of Wolves* and the short stories it is based upon.

STALKING FROM THE SILVER SCREEN

Recurring as it does throughout folklore and literature, it was only a matter of time before the werewolf found its way into cinema. Interestingly, the werewolf's first cinematic outing also marked the first filmic appearance of the female werewolf, a figure who, until relatively recently, was often overlooked in cinema (see '**A She-Wolf Came…**'). While now believed to be a lost film, destroyed in a fire in 1924, *The Werewolf* (1913) tells of a Navajo witch-woman whose daughter transforms into a wolf to seek revenge on the white settlers who killed her father. It was directed by Canadian film-maker Henry MacRae, who amongst other things is credited as pioneering the use of artificial light for interior filming and the use of double exposures in early cinema. The screenplay was written by Ruth Ann Baldwin, a former journalist, and is very loosely based on Henry Beaugrand's short story 'The Werewolves' (1898), which tells of a band of pioneers who believe there are (Native American) werewolves prowling around outside their snowbound Canadian fort; an idea also echoed in Grant Harvey's *Ginger Snaps Back: The Beginning* (2004).

Unlike the vampire, the classic cinematic representation of which stems directly from Stoker's *Dracula*, the werewolf lacks a singular classic text or literary source from which any strong influence extends. While Guy Endore's *The Werewolf of Paris* had a large influence over werewolf cinema, many film-makers, including Neil Jordan, drew inspiration not only from folklore, but from several specific film titles that preceded the groundbreaking werewolf films of the Eighties. According to Bourgault du Coudray, these earlier titles 'forged a new synthesis'[8] of mythology concerning the werewolf, introducing elements now considered standard conventions of the werewolf film, such as the contagious nature of lycanthropy, the influence of the full moon on the werewolf's transformations, and the use of silver to exterminate lycanthropes. One of these titles is Stuart Walker's *Werewolf of London* (1935). While travelling through Tibet in search of a mysterious flower that blooms under moonlight, renowned botanist Wilfred Glendon (Henry Hull) is attacked by a strange creature. When he returns to London, Glendon begins to undergo a terrifying transformation, the only antidote for which appears to be the plant he is researching. Produced by Universal in the wake of the success of *Dracula* (1931), *Frankenstein* (1931) and *The Mummy* (1932), *Werewolf of London* was the first mainstream Hollywood werewolf film. Heavily influenced by Guy Endore's *The Werewolf of Paris*, it established several other important precedents, such as the tragic male protagonist and the spiritual torment he suffers as he desperately attempts to find a cure for his condition as the eponymous beast. It also introduced the idea that lycanthropy is contagious, a notion that did not really exist in literature or folklore. The make-up effects by Jack Pierce transformed actor Henry Hull into a therianthropic man-wolf hybrid, the look of which echoed throughout later werewolf films, notably George Waggner's highly influential *The Wolf Man* (1941), which further congealed and popularised certain conventions established by *Werewolf of London*, as well as Mike Nichols's *Wolf* (1994).

Written by Curt Siodmak, a friend of Guy Endore, Waggner's film further solidified the idea of lycanthropy as a markedly masculine struggle with the 'beast within'. After the sudden death of his brother, Larry Talbot (Lon Chaney) returns to his ancestral home in Wales and is reunited with his father (Claude Rains). Talbot befriends local shopkeeper Gwen (Evelyn Ankers), and as they take a moonlit stroll through the woods, he is attacked by a wolf-like creature (Bela Lugosi), whose gypsy mother (Maria Ouspenskaya) reveals to be a werewolf. During the next full moon, Talbot undergoes a horrifying transformation and after terrorising the village is eventually killed by his own father. Many subsequent werewolf films took their lead from *The Wolf Man*, with its depiction of a doomed hero who suffers psychological trauma when infected with lycanthropy and attempts to save himself and those he loves from the claws of his inner monster. Waggner's film also popularised the use of silver to exterminate werewolves, and the idea of the full moon as an influencing force in lycanthropy, though this idea was more fully developed in Roy William Neil's sequel, *Frankenstein Meets The Wolf Man* (1943). In that film's beautifully eerie opening scene, in which the crypt of Larry Talbot is invaded by thieves, the cascading rays of the moon pour over Talbot's exhumed body, resurrecting him, and his dormant inner beast.

The Wolf Man also helped to establish the Freudian psychoanalytical aspects of the werewolf in cinema. According to Darryl Jones, Talbot's transformation into a man-beast exhibits 'an outward projection of the obvious sexual frustration he feels' in his relationship with Gwen, and that a 'riot of phallic symbolism' occurs during the film's climax, when Talbot's domineering father beats him to death with a silver-headed cane.[9] RKO's *Cat People* (1942), a feline variation of the werewolf film, was produced to cash in on the popularity of *The Wolf Man*. Producer Val Lewton and director Jacques Tourneur crafted a thoughtful, literary tale that picked up the trail of psychosexual anxiety and beastly transformation of Waggner's film, albeit in a much more restrained manner. Indeed, *Cat People* was one of the first films to directly reference the work of Sigmund Freud, and it unfurls as a darkly suggestive study of sexual repression and the horrors it can unleash. It tells of Irena (Simone Simon), a young Serbian fashion designer whose marriage to the all-American Oliver (Kent Smith) becomes increasingly strained when they fail to consummate their marital bonds. Irena believes she is descended from a race of satanic cat people, doomed to transform into a ravaging panther when aroused. Matters become further complicated when Oliver begins an affair with his co-worker Alice (Jane Randolph), and Irena's heartbreak and jealously unlocks a side of her she had previously tried to suppress. The ambiguity of *Cat People* would find its way into *She-Wolf of London* (1946), which tells of the psychological turmoil of a vulnerable young woman (June Lockhart) whose scheming relatives attempt to convince her she is a werewolf and is responsible for several brutal murders. The unleashing of animalistic sexuality coupled with beastly transformation is also rife throughout Terence Fisher's *The Curse of the Werewolf*. Oliver Reed stars as Leon Corledo, a man conceived by rape and born on Christmas Day. Leon is adopted by a kind-hearted couple, but as he grows so

Tearing skin

Fangs

too do his strangely violent urges. While his morbid tendencies are calmed by his love for Christina (Catherine Feller), his fate is sealed because of his brutal heritage and he eventually transforms into a werewolf, terrorising his village before being killed by his father.

ENTER THE COMPANY OF WOLVES

Lore surrounding the werewolf would continue to evolve with its cinematic representation. The idea of werewolves as cursed individuals, evoking connotations of unavoidable tragedy and doomed inevitability, would gradually give way to a more positive identification that recognised the connections between manhood and primal nature.

The Company of Wolves was produced at a time when several other werewolf films had recently made a distinct impression on horror cinema. John Landis's *An American Werewolf in London* and Joe Dante's *The Howling* reinvented the cinematic werewolf with their ground-breaking special effects depicting painful onscreen transformations in ways previously unimaginable, 'in which the human body is radically figured and disfigured as a site of horror'.[11] John Landis's classic tells of American college students David (David Naughton) and Jack (Griffin Dunne), who are backpacking through rural England when they are attacked by a large wolf. Jack is killed in the attack and a severely mutilated David awakens in hospital. He is plagued by violent visions of his dead friend who warns David that he is becoming a werewolf and should 'Beware the moon'. During the next full moon, David begins a grisly transformation from man to bloodthirsty beast in a scene, still highly revered, showcasing Rick Baker's astonishing make-up effects.

Released in the same year and adapted from Gary Brandner's 1977 novel, *The Howling* featured similarly impressive transformation sequences unflinching in their painful details. When TV reporter Karen White (Dee Wallace) survives an attempt on her life whilst aiding the police in their arrest of a serial killer, her therapist packs her off to an isolated psychiatric retreat. Much to her horror, Karen eventually discovers that the other residents are all werewolves and her adulterous husband has also become one. Of the various werewolf films released in the early eighties, *The Company of Wolves* perhaps shares most in common with *The Howling*. Dante's film also depicts the werewolf as a 'figuration of lust'[12] by paralleling sexuality and lycanthropy. The werewolves residing in the rural commune are undergoing therapy and attempting to repress the animal inside. They eventually give up their attempts to channel primal instincts because, as one character insists, 'You can't tame what's meant to be wild, doc. It just ain't natural.' The film also begins with a 'surfeit of sexual imagery'[13] as Karen visits a downtown sex shop to help police detectives capture rapist and serial killer, Eddie Quist (Robert Picardo). As she views a graphic film with him in a private booth, he 'wolfs out' as he appears to become increasingly aroused. Later, Karen's husband Bill (Christopher Stone), a sensitive, 'New Age' vegetarian, quickly develops an insatiable appetite for meat and sex when, during an illicit rendezvous with the predatory Marsha (Elisabeth Brooks), he is bitten by her and infected with lycanthropy. According to Gregory Waller, 'by venturing into the moonlight and acting upon his desires, Bill becomes a werewolf; in and through sex, the beast within emerges'.[14]

Also released in 1981 was Michael Wadleigh's *Wolfen*. An adaptation of Whitley Strieber's debut novel *The Wolfen* (1978), it follows Dewey Wilson (Albert Finney), a New York City detective investigating a series of grisly deaths seemingly caused by a ferocious wild beast. He and his partner, Rebecca Neff (Diane Venora), are warned by a group of inner-city Native Americans that the attacks are perpetrated by mythical wolf-like creatures known as Wolfen. With its themes regarding mankind's brutal impact on the environment, *Wolfen* parallels the plight of the Native Americans with that of the titular creatures, who have taken increasingly violent measures to protect their territory: a derelict neighbourhood in The Bronx that is being systematically demolished to make way for plush apartment buildings. According to Roger Ebert, it isn't so much a werewolf film as a film 'about the possibility that Indians and wolves can exchange souls'.[15]

TRANSFORMATIONS

The Company of Wolves stands outside this pack of films, not only due to its lack of adherence to certain established conventions, but also because it presented the figure of the werewolf from the perspective of a dreaming girl. It is more concerned with using the werewolf as a metaphor for adult sexuality and the fascination and terror it provokes within the girl. It avoids a 'traditional' werewolf narrative which, in the words of Bourgault du Coudray, usually follows the male protagonist's 'confusion, denial [...] abortive attempts to control or curve his condition, spiritual torment, desperate efforts to warn potential victims of their danger, despair and tragic death'.[16] However, Jordan was still mindful that his film needed to satisfy audiences already primed by the spectacular 'body-horror' effects of other recent werewolf titles. There are three major transformation scenes throughout *The Company of Wolves*, all of which were rigorously storyboarded after extensive discussions. Jordan was keen to avoid depicting therianthropic man-wolf hybrids such as those seen in the likes of *The Wolf Man* and *The Howling*, and opted to convey the transformation of a man into an actual wolf. He also felt it was important to imbue his creatures with pathos, as the transformations in Carter's original stories had a 'sadness about them, and a sensuality as if the heroes cannot resist that wolf inside them, and as if the wolf always longs to be human again'.[17] While they retain a certain tragic quality akin to the spiritually tortured creatures of

The Wolf Man and its ilk, the melancholy of Jordan's monsters stems from their being misunderstood and shunned by society. They are seen as devilish and immoral because they indulge in flesh and desire, they do not deny their natural impulses. The werewolves in *The Company of Wolves* represent adult sexuality as viewed by an adolescent girl. Her perceptions are formed by the nightmarish stories told to her by her Granny, an unrelentingly pious woman from a much older generation with much harsher opinions on such matters. According to Granny, the worst wolves, which are hairy on the inside, drag you to hell with them and offer nothing but eternal damnation. Granny not only sees them as a horror that threatens the body, but the very soul. Rosaleen's outlook begins to change as she crosses the threshold from childhood to adulthood and when she begins to acknowledge her own sexual desires. She eventually loses the innocence of childhood, reflected in the strangely melancholic aura that imbues the werewolves in her dreams. This atmosphere of sadness and mourning for lost childhood combines with her newly awakened sensuality, but also with dread and repulsion as she struggles to reconcile what she has been told by her Granny, with what she feels and knows in her own heart. The empathy and terror evoked by Jordan's lycanthropes not only highlight their morbid sensuality by entwining the terrifying with the sublime, but creates what Zucker refers to as a 'mythic reciprocity of beauty and terror […] a subject common to Jordan's films'.[18] Jordan claimed *The Company of Wolves* was to be *about* sex, not about *hating* it[19] and as such, he was keen to avoid depicting anything too repulsive. According to Robin Wood, 'the release of sexuality in the horror film is always presented as perverted, monstrous and excessive; both the perversion and the excess being the logical outcome of repression'.[20] Jordan wanted to celebrate the release of sexuality and cited the imagery in films like *Alien* and *The Thing* (1982), which he believed conveyed 'a very deep hatred of sexuality, a pathological disgust with the human form […]',[21] as something he wanted to avoid wallowing in.

The transformation sequences were created by Christopher Tucker, a former opera singer who had designed the astonishing make-up effects for David Lynch's *The Elephant Man* (1980). According to Jordan, it was Tucker who suggested the wolves should emerge through the mouths of the transforming characters, accentuating the idea of the 'beast within'. Jordan noted, 'in a world where a Covent Garden baritone can end up designing monsters, I suppose anything can happen'.[22] They tested a series of ideas involving peeling skin and a mouth in an 'anguished cry [with] a wolf emerging through it'.[23] When designing the effects in the scene where the bridegroom (Stephen Rea) returns home and transforms into a wolf by tearing off his own skin, in order to replicate muscular structures underneath the skin which, according to Jordan, possess a strange beauty, he and Tucker looked to Leonardo da Vinci's anatomical drawings and certain portraits by Francis Bacon. The monster Rea changes into was operated by several people kneeling beneath the camera, and his flayed visage prefigures certain imagery from Clive Barker's *Hellraiser* (1987). Indeed, Barker echoed Jordan's sentiments when he suggested 'for some of us, monsters are welcome opportunities to be different, to act in anti-normal ways, hideous and beautiful at the same time'.[23] The combination of sensuality and terror is most powerful during the scene in which the Huntsman transforms into a wolf before Rosaleen's very eyes. Jordan had initially planned more effects for this scene, including hairs sprouting wildly across the man's bared flesh, however he realised that because of the actor's background in movement and dance, he had the ability to writhe and contort his body in grotesque and fascinating ways. As the Huntsman transforms in front of Granny's glowing hearth, the light from the fire casts shadows along the rippling contours of his back, creating a striking image; the strange sensuality of which implies so much.

While the presence of the moon is strong throughout *The Company of Wolves*, it doesn't appear to initiate transformation. In Jordan's film, human to lupine metamorphoses seem to occur when emotions are heightened, such as the scene in which the bridegroom turns into a wolf after accusing his former wife of adultery, and the moment when the Huntsman is shot by Rosaleen. In the story Rosaleen tells her mother, the wedding party is cursed by a vengeful witch, while her second story, told to the Huntsman, tells of a wolf-girl who 'strayed from the path' into the forest of flesh and desire. Lycanthropy stems as much from the result of succumbing to carnal impulses, as it is an outer signifier of the inner workings of those who stray from the path.

FOOTNOTES

1.   Carter (1995) p118
2.   Bourgault du Coudray (2006) p2

3. Bourgault du Coudray (2006) p5
4. Duncan (2013) p29
5. Sconduto (2008) pg9
6. Cited in Frost (2003) p76
7. Frost (2003) p150
8. Bourgault du Coudray (2006) p76
9. Jones (2002) p171
10. Jones (2002) p75
11. Bourgault du Coudray (2006) p115
12. Bourgault du Coudray (2006) p84
13. ibid.
14. ibid.
15. http://www.rogerebert.com/reviews/wolfen-1981
16. Bourgault du Coudray (2006) p76
17. Zucker (2013) p43
18. Zucker (2013) p4
19. Zucker (2013) p44
20. Wood (2003) p82
21. Zucker (2013) pp43-44
22. ibid.
23. Jones (2002) p75

CHAPTER SIX: 'A SHE-WOLF CAME...'

'I'm a goddamn force of nature.' Ginger, *Ginger Snaps* (2000)

Throughout history werewolves have traditionally been a masculinised beast associated with cultural concepts of masculinity. Even the word 'werewolf' is gendered; 'were' is Old English for 'male' and 'werewolf' literally translates as 'man wolf'. When using the figure of the wolf as an analogy to describe human characteristics, it is still quite gendered; 'alpha male' and 'pack leader' are connotative of male dominance and aggression, and predatory males are often referred to as 'wolves'. *The Company of Wolves* is an atypical werewolf film as it uses the figure of the lycanthrope to explore notions of adult sexuality from a distinctly feminine vantage point: from within the dreams of an adolescent girl. Throughout the film werewolves are not only sexualised, but feminised. Monsters sinister *and* sensual, they provoke feelings of terror, fascination and desire within Rosaleen. The story she tells the Huntsman features a wolf-girl who mirrors Rosaleen's own inner beast and, in the words of medieval scholar and editor of *She-Wolf: A Cultural History of Female Werewolves* (2015), Hannah Priest, acts as a 'dark double'[1] to Rosaleen. Indeed, Carter stated that her wolves carried allegorical weight, and that they signified libido, projected desires and the sexual drive of women. She described *The Company of Wolves* as a 'menstrual film'[2] in which the wolves 'stand for the girl's own sexuality, rather than rough, hairy male sexuality – perhaps they stand for rough hairy female sexuality'.[3] In light of this symbolic nature of the film, Priest suggests, 'It's hard to argue that there's really a "werewolf" in *The Company of Wolves*, as so much of what we see is a thinly-veiled allegory for something else. However, that's not a criticism, as werewolves – particularly female werewolves – have been used as the vehicle to discuss various 'human' anxieties for many centuries. Sometimes a werewolf is just a werewolf, but quite often it's a metaphor.'[4] It's this specific, unconventional use of the werewolf that separates Jordan's film from much of its ilk.

According to Pramaggiore, Rosaleen's encounter with and subsequent seduction of the Huntsman, as well as her off-screen transformation into a wolf, is a very significant and influential moment, not only in the film but in the history of horror cinema.[5] It challenges the traditional representation of the werewolf as inherently masculine. When the Huntsman transforms into a wolf in Granny's cottage, his body turns inside out as he literally births a wolf from his mouth. In an uncanny reversal of traditional sexual imagery, the wolf's muzzle emerging from his mouth can be seen as a depiction of 'a phallus emerging from (rather than entering) a vaginal cavity'.[6] As well as feminising its monsters, *The Company of Wolves* also features the presence of not one but two female werewolves: the wolf-girl from Rosaleen's story, who is described by Rosaleen as a girl who ventured from the path and remembered what she saw there, and Rosaleen herself, whose own fate is anticipated in the aforementioned story of the wolf-girl.

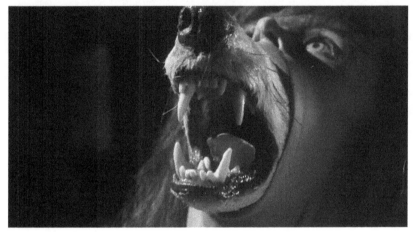

The wolf within

While female werewolves are much rarer in cinema than their male counterparts, in folk stories and literature they have a long history and association with nature, the earth and the unleashing of formidable sexuality. Rosaleen's sexual awakening is explored in her dreamscape, a dense forest populated with werewolves – forests and wolves are both symbols of nature and transformation, and throughout the film's narrative they enable transition from culture to nature and masculine to feminine, respectively. Priest suggests the history of the female werewolf is rather non-linear, and while it is impossible to chart its progression from early texts, it *is* possible to identify key motifs in how she has been depicted. One such motif common to the female werewolf is her sexualisation. Markedly different from her male counterpart, the female werewolf is usually embracing of her condition; more precisely, embracing of the power it imbues her with. According to Jancovich, the 'physical processes of transformation […] not only threaten engulfment and assimilation, but they also offer the possibility of liberation and power from the conventional limits of the body and the self'.[7]

FEARSOME FEMININITY

Since the Enlightenment, women and femininity have been positioned as a marked 'other' to men and masculinity. Whereas masculinity was aligned with culture and reason, femininity came to be associated with nature and biology. Female sexuality in particular was regarded as so feral and animalistic it was deemed completely unacceptable and must therefore be suppressed; the virtue of virginity was advocated as a way to control women. As Dorinda Outram explains, it was believed that the female temperament was controlled by nature, not by reason: 'Increasingly, medical writings seemed to imply that women were virtually a separate species within the human race, characterised by their reproductive functions, and by a sexuality which was often denied or repressed.'[8] These same medical writings referred to capricious animal 'humours' or vapours rising from the womb to the brain and resulting in women being biologically incapable of transcending basic instincts and controlling their nature. Historically, the term 'hysteria' referred to a medical condition believed to be specific to women and was linked to childbirth and the uterus, the Greek word for which was 'hystera'. Hippocrates wrote of the 'wandering womb' and described it as 'an animal within an animal' capable of sentience and mobility. It was thought virgins were particularly vulnerable to hysteria resulting from menstrual blood, the only cure for which was to become pregnant.

Woman's marked difference from man took on monstrous qualities such as the idea of the vagina dentata (toothed vagina), with its connotations of a ravenous and beastly appetite. In the words of Sigmund Freud, 'No male human being is spared the terrifying shock of threatened castration at the sight of the female genitals'.[9] Indeed, many cultures share a conception of what Barbara Creed refers to as the 'monstrous feminine':[10] the Greek word for semen ('sema') not only means 'seed', but also 'food'. The Yanomamos of South America used a word meaning 'pregnant' which also meant 'satiated' and 'full-fed'. Their word meaning 'to eat' was the same as 'to copulate'. Old Muslim aphorisms stated that only three things were insatiable: the desert, the grave and a woman's vulva. The Anglo-Saxon word for 'mouth' ('muth') stems from the same root as the word for 'mother'. Vulvas are even described as having 'labia' (lips). As Zucker notes, 'It is not coincidental that in Italian the word for male wolf is lupo, and lupa, the word for female wolf, also means vulva'.[11]

Gorgons, sirens, sphinxes, witches, harpies and myriad other female monsters from myths and legends around the world were depicted as hideously alluring, wielding formidable sexuality with which they conquered and castrated male foes. This 'othering' of the female body, with its pairing of the monstrous and the feminine, found its way into tales of female werewolves who, due to their links with nature, blood and biology, were more often than not depicted as hedonistic, seductive and utterly revelling in their condition. Kirby Flower Smith suggests, 'As the wolf is the symbol of unbridled cruelty so, in Roman Parlance, the she-wolf [...] represented unbridled lust'.[12] They represent the unleashing of female sexuality and empowerment, which contrasts strongly with male lycanthropy and man's psychological struggle to suppress the beast within.

For centuries the grim fates of many female werewolves in literature and cinema have spoken of the deep-rooted cultural admonition regarding the expression of women's desire and sexuality, the very notion of which has been standardised and perpetuated by fairy tales like Red Riding Hood. The female werewolf has been regarded as a sexual menace that must be exterminated because of her threat to order in society. While male werewolves are generally depicted as desperately seeking redemption and a cure for their monthly transformations, for female werewolves there is usually no hope of redemption because they embrace the release lycanthropy affords them. One need only look to recent depictions of the female werewolf such as Marsha in Joe Dante's *The Howling* and Ginger in *Ginger Snaps* to be reminded of Rosaleen's mother's remark regarding the beast in men finding its match in women. Indeed, certain dialogue in Dante's film humorously foregrounds Marsha's incarnation of powerful female sexuality and its links with nature. According to Dr Waggner, 'We could all learn a great deal from Marsha. She's a very elemental person. It's all that natural energy.' Another character suddenly interjects, retorting, 'She's a nymphomaniac!'

According to Bourgault du Coudray, it was believed to be more natural for women to become werewolves than men, and lycanthropy in women was a 'consequence of a feminine tendency towards pleasure of the flesh'.[13] In other words, it was believed women – because of their inherent sensuality – were more susceptible to Satanic temptation than men. Indeed, Christian doctrine places the blame for The Fall of humanity on the shoulders of the first woman, Eve, and her succumbing to temptation. When she was unable to resist looking back at the destruction of Sodom and Gomorrah, Lot's inquisitive wife was punished by God and transformed into a pillar of salt. In Greek mythology, the evils and ills of mankind were blamed on Pandora whose curiosity led her to open a magic box she was forbidden to unlock. In certain versions of the fairy tale of Bluebeard, his wife loses her life when she peeps inside the forbidden chamber. Female curiosity and imagery connotative of the loss of innocence through sexual temptation, such as snakes coiled about the branches of trees, and glimpses of gleaming red apples, glints throughout The Company of Wolves to serve as a reminder of the choices Rosaleen must make in acknowledging her desires. According to Zipes, when the Catholic Church and the Protestant reformation combined their fire and brimstone efforts to rationalise society and rid it of social deviants, women in particular were linked to potentially uncontrollable natural instincts associated with the Devil. He goes on to note that, 'as the image of the innocent, naïve child susceptible to wild natural forces arose, the necessity to control and shelter children became more pronounced'.[14] This resulted in witch and werewolf trials to punish those accused of non-conformism. According to H.R. Trevor-Roper, many were executed to deliberately arouse fear and anxiety in society while new 'models of male and female behaviour were created to exalt a more ascetic way of life'.[15]

FEMALE WEREWOLVES IN LITERATURE

According to Priest, the earliest account of female lycanthropy is found in Gerald of Wales's twelfth century Topographia Hiberniae, and her metamorphosis from human to animal is revealed to be the result of a divine curse inflicted as expiation for sin. One of the first literary female werewolves made her appearance in 'The Werewolf', a short story extracted from Frederick Marryat's novel The Phantom Ship (1839). The segment, which has been published in myriad anthologies and re-titled 'The White Wolf of the Hartz Mountains' is, according to Frost, highly significant as it introduced an erotic element to its depiction of the werewolf as a seductive and alluring woman. The erotic element would be expanded upon by Clemence Housman, an accomplished engraver and leading figure in the British Suffragette movement, in her ground-breaking novella *The Were-Wolf* (1896). Housman's beautifully wrought tale of an isolated community infiltrated by a mysterious woman named White Fell, boasts a snowy, Nordic setting, a formidable and dangerously alluring female werewolf, and is awash with Christian allegory. In the words of Robert Reginald and Robert Menville, 'No one has treated lycanthropy with more beauty or literacy'[16] than Housman, whose tale was described by Frost as a classic of the late nineteenth century.[17] According to H.P. Lovecraft, it 'attains a high degree of gruesome tension and achieves to some extent the atmosphere of authentic folklore'.[18]

Other significant titles featuring female werewolves are Madame Aino Kallas' *The Wolf's Bride* (1930), a novel which tells of a hunter's wife who is cursed by a forest demon to become a wolf, and Arlton Eadie's 'The Wolf-Girl of Josselin' (1938). Eadie's short story tells of a young beggar woman who avenges the death of her infant son by cursing the cruel women of the village who denied her food and shelter and transforming them into werewolves. In later years the titular character, a descendent of one of the women of Josselin, manages to break the curse when her maternal instincts win over her more predatory inclinations. Eadie's story is significant because it marked a shift in the representation of the female werewolf; conveying her in a positive light, it fore-grounded the she-wolf's protective maternal instincts. There are certain parallels between this story and the wedding party segment in *The Company of Wolves*, in which a woman exacts revenge by cursing those who have wronged her and transforms them into wolves. Some of Carter's other stories from *The Bloody Chamber* would echo Seabury Quinn's 'The Gentle Werewolf' (1940), a short story that subverts typical 'animal bridegroom' fairy tale conventions with its depiction of a maiden transformed into a wolf by a vengeful witch. The maiden must remain a wolf until a noble lord falls in love with her. She eventually rescues a former suitor who kisses her and breaks the curse. Manly Banister's 'Eena' (1947) also subverted typical werewolf story conventions with its she-wolf who becomes a human woman during the full moon.

Female lycanthropy as the result of tainted heritage occurs in Franklin Gregory's novel *The White Wolf* (1941), which follows the exploits of a wealthy businessman's daughter who, in the form of a white wolf, goes on a killing spree. It is revealed her involvement in a Satanic cult and her subsequent fate were predestined because of an ancestor's pact with the Devil. Grace M. Campbell's 'The Law of the Hills' (1930) tells of a bride who succumbs to hereditary lycanthropy, while S.R. Crockett's historical romance The Black Douglas (1899) features a female werewolf who procures children for sacrifice at Black Masses. The antagonist from Count Eric Stenbock's 'The Other Side' (1893) also poses a threat to the young. She entices a village boy into the forest before revealing her true self to him: 'Among the deep blue flowers walked one with long gleaming golden hair […] But when a cloud passed over the moon he saw no beautiful woman but a wolf.'[19]

One of the most significant female werewolves in contemporary literature appears in science-fiction and fantasy author Suzy McKee Charnas's award-winning short story, 'Boobs' (1989). With its awkward teenaged protagonist and its amalgamation of lycanthropy and ambivalent female adolescence, 'Boobs' shares strong affinities with The Company of Wolves and preceded the thematically similar Ginger Snaps by over a decade. It tells of Kelsey, a shy and lonely teenager whose menarche coincides with her transformation into a wolf. She uses her new-found power and abilities to take revenge on a menacing bully who has made her life a living hell and whose cruel nickname for Kelsey, due to her developing body, is the title of the story.

As with a great deal of McKee Charnas's work, 'Boobs' draws upon and subverts folk and fairy story tropes. Her heroine, like those who appear in the pages of Carter's work, is curious and doesn't shirk from exploring new sensory experiences brought about by her transforming body and the power it imbues her with. 'I read a great deal of folk and fairy tales and mythology as a young person,' the author explains. 'It soaks into your brain. I did some deliberate things, intentional subversions of the folk tropes: the stepmother, for example, isn't "wicked" — she's realistic, and trying to help. Kelsey herself doesn't know anything about werewolves except what she's seen in horror movies, and she's glad to throw herself into the sensory rewards of her new body rather than hiding in her room and being scared and worried about hurting people. She's found power and she dares to use it, which goes against stories like the girl who spins straw into gold, so she's exploited by greedy people and bullied by a goblin.'[20]

Like many female werewolves, Kelsey embraces and celebrates her power and according to McKee Charnas, the story was inspired by an incident from her own childhood.

I'd been reading about bullying in schools, and it reminded me of some experiences of my own back in my own school days. We now understand (I think) that bullying is a form of violence, and women at every age still have to try to figure out how to deal with the kinds of violence routinely directed at them, often by other women as well, but that wasn't so much on my mind at the time. The idea of simply reversing the physical strength dynamic really appealed to me, so that's what I wrote about [...] I wanted to become stronger, faster, and more dangerous, so I could hit back effectively and make them think twice about hitting someone smaller and weaker than they were. Kelsey becomes a wolf to do that, and of course it feels good! It's not complicated. She could have done the same to a girl bully who attacked her, but being strong enough to overcome the muscular differences between average boys and average girls was the important point: to hit back and *make it hurt*. To win over your own body's hormonal treachery – who *wouldn't* celebrate that?[21]

RECONNECTING WITH NATURE

Just as the meaning of the tale of Red Riding Hood has changed and evolved throughout history, with each reinterpretation reflecting certain cultural values, so too have representations of the werewolf, particularly the female werewolf, changed over time. In the words of Bourgault du Coudray, 'material relating to the werewolf in every period has been informed by prevailing cultural values and dominant ways of knowing or speaking about the world'.[22] With every successive generation, the cultural values and ideologies that inform the representation of the werewolf are subject to change. In more recent times, the werewolf and its links with nature have been depicted in an increasingly positive light. According to Priest, this 'hypersexualised' female werewolf finds its most developed expression in the fiction, cinema and television of the late 20th century and early 21st century, 'where traditions of animalistic female nature combine with medieval notions of the perfidious female, Victorian Gothic tropes of the supernatural seductress, the film noir's femme fatale and anxieties surrounding "sex-positive" post-feminism'.[23] During the Seventies and Eighties there were a number of women writers – including Carter, Tanith Lee, Marion Zimmer Bradley and Suzy McKee Charnas to name but a few – who drew on mythology and symbolism pertaining to

The She-wolf

the feminine as a means to attain female empowerment and challenge the detrimental positioning of woman as man's 'other'. According to McKee Charnas, 'There's a good deal of modern fiction, most of it by women authors, that picks up fairy tale tropes and kicks the stuffing out of them to see what's in there besides rules to tame and control girls. Angela Carter famously worked this material, but there are many others. Even the familiar Disney B.S. about princesses and mermaids, etc. gets challenged now. Some of the female "superheroes" of comics and TV series are attempts to turn misogynistic fairy tales on their heads, and youth culture seems ready to embrace that, I'm glad to say.'[24] In the Nineties, this continued with the likes of Clarissa Pinkola Estes's *Women Who Run With the Wolves* (1992) – a compendium of stories and essays exploring the archetype of the Wild Woman – and feminist author and neo-paganist Barbara G. Walker's *Amazon: A Novel* (1992), which tells of an Amazonian warrior who finds herself in twentieth-century New Jersey. It offers a piercing critique of patriarchal society while extolling the matrilineal values of the titular character's community. Walker's *Feminist Fairy Tales* (1996), a collection of Carter-esque reinterpretations of classic fairy tales, followed several years later. Bourgault du Coudray considers works such as these to be part of the 'valorisation' of the feminine and suggests they surged against the distortion of the feminine under patriarchal dominance.

While stories which invite sympathy for the werewolf aren't new, they have become an increasingly common aspect of werewolf literature and cinema. As authors began to explore alternative notions of selfhood and womanhood, links between the lycanthrope's monthly cycle and female menstruation began to emerge to create stories concerning the empowerment of women. This was largely as a result of feminist views towards menstruation insisting it should be celebrated as a fundamental aspect of womanhood, not smothered in shame. Parallels between menstruation and lycanthropy were connected by Walter Evans in 1973 when he suggested 'the werewolf's bloody attacks – which occur regularly every month – are certainly related to the menstrual cycle which suddenly and mysteriously commands the body of every adolescent girl'.[25] Barbara Creed also suggested the figure of the werewolf was inherently feminised because of its ability 'to give birth to himself, in either animal or human form, at the time of the full moon or once a month [...] Like the woman with her menstrual cycle, the werewolf replenishes his blood monthly and is reborn monthly'.[26] While there is a long tradition of the links between the menstrual cycle and lunar activity, parallels between lycanthropy and menstruation are a relatively recent notion. According to Louise Watson, 'the recurring motif of the full moon draws obvious parallels between the menstrual (often thought lunar) cycle and the "call of the wild" of the full moon for werewolves'.[27] This notion resides at the heart of McKee Charnas's short story 'Boobs', and the author noted:

> The whole werewolf thing is grounded in our ideas about civilization vs. wildness – the human and the Beast, and how people can slip from one state to the other and back again [...] More specifically, though, the werewolf concept is strongly grounded in our *idea* of wildness, which is one of becoming totally absorbed in the present, in our own immediate appetites and desires, which of course includes sexual desires. Since adolescence is so powerfully infused with sexual impulses (or worries about *not* having sexual impulses, or having the wrong ones), that's a powerful connection to the idea of the wolf-side of the personality, the raw Id freed from human convention and morality.[28]

As such, *The Company of Wolves* and the short stories it is based upon can be seen as important precursors to the feminist reclamation of the werewolf in titles such as 'Boobs', 'Wolfland' (1983) by Tanith Lee, *Blood and Chocolate* (1997) by Annette Curtis

Klause, and, perhaps most significantly, John Fawcett's cult film *Ginger Snaps* (2000), all of which parallel lycanthropy and menstruation in order to explore ideas regarding female adolescence, subjective agency and autonomy.

GROWING PAINS

In her critique on *Carrie* (1976), one of the most powerful films concerning the horror of female adolescence, Shelley Stamp noted '[the] adolescent body becomes the site upon which monster and victim converge',[29] a statement that easily applies itself to the plight of the werewolf. Evans argued that the werewolf could be seen as specifically representing the terrors of puberty: 'clearly the monster offers the sexually confused adolescent a sympathetic, and at best a tragic, imitation of his life by representing a mysterious and irreversible change which forever isolates him from what he identifies as normality, security, and goodness, a change thrusting him into a world he does not understand, torturing him with desires he cannot satisfy or even admit, a world in which dark psychological and strange physical changes seem to conspire with society to destroy him'.[30] While titles such as *I Was a Teenage Werewolf* (1957), *Teen Wolf* (1985) and *Full Moon High* (1981) used lycanthropy as a metaphor for the onset of male adolescent sexuality, with links drawn between physical changes in the body, the sprouting of excess body hair and the surge in uncontrollable libidinous impulses, it has rarely been presented from a young woman's perspective.

According to Jancovich, ideas concerning lycanthropic transformation and body-horror are actually inherently feminine as they relate to notions of 'the body as womb'.[31] *The Company of Wolves* is significant because it not only utilises the figure of the werewolf to explore ideas regarding female sexuality, but female *adolescent* sexuality. It is a film about sexual awakening, a coming of age parable charting the figurative and literal transformation of a young girl as she leaves childhood behind and becomes an adult. As Hannah Priest explains, 'The Company of Wolves is very much of its time, both in terms of style and message. However, as far as female werewolves go, I think there's a case for arguing that it was very influential on later texts, or, perhaps, on ideas more generally. The relationship between female werewolves and sexuality is really cemented in the 19th century, though there are hints of an association in earlier texts, particularly in some reports of witchcraft. *The Company of Wolves* undoubtedly draws on that – via Carter's short stories – as well as on the association of the Little Red Riding Hood story with burgeoning female sexual identity, which really only happens in the late 20th century'.[32]

Carter drew upon the connection between lycanthropy and female coming of age marked by the onset of menstruation that renders Red Riding Hood a narrative concerned with female puberty. *The Company of Wolves* delves into female sexuality and, in its exploration of culturally constructed forbidden femininity, tells of the very real horrors of growing up female. According to McKee Charnas:

> So much of our fiction for young readers and viewers is about the tribulations of pubescent boys – feeling inadequate and not able to compete, coping with crazy new energies and the highs of being part of this or that crowd of guys (or *not* being accepted by other boys, and being bullied for being different, or perceived as weak, etc.). Everybody has versions of typical puberty as boys and girls experience it pressed on them from all sides by the entertainment industry as well as by their own experiences. The real differences are stark, though: girls are at greater risk, physically and emotionally, from bullies of both sexes because girls are routinely, publicly shamed for showing strength, are called 'bitches' for being assertive or 'too smart', and generally put down for aspiring to adult autonomy. Sometimes it's better, sometimes it's worse — race, class, and other factors all influence how this plays out — but any girl with a brain knows early on that the future she can hope to attain is 'less' in so many ways that what the boys can hope for. Look in today's *New York Times*: there's an article about why the gender gap in pay in America remains stubbornly high […] You don't have to make this shit up. It's there in our history.[33]

Through notions of blood and monthly changes instigated by the moon, Carter intimately connects the ambivalent figure of the pubescent girl, fluctuating between childhood and adulthood, with the figure of the werewolf, which fluctuates between human and beast. Priest suggests that what *The Company of Wolves* does is 'draw a direct parallel between adolescence, developing sexual identity and the female werewolf – and this is an idea that has really become embedded in the popular imagination. Much of this is derived from Carter's reimagining of folk and fairy tales, but the film's aesthetic develops the association even further, for example the visual linking of Rosaleen's red lipstick and spotted nightshirt with the red flowers and red cloak, and – by association – with menstrual blood. This association has proved to be highly influential'.[34]

As mentioned, The Company of Wolves and the parallels it draws between adolescence, menstruation, lycanthropy and female sexuality, is an immensely significant precursor to John Fawcett's cult film Ginger Snaps. The most significant cinematic 'menstrual horror' since Carrie, Ginger Snaps was written by Karen Walton, whose script deftly parallels the painful bodily transformations of puberty with those of lycanthropy from a distinctly feminine perspective. The film tells of two morbid teenaged sisters, Ginger (Katherine Isabelle) and Brigitte (Emily Perkins) Fitzgerald. On the night she begins to menstruate, Ginger is attacked by a werewolf and gradually begins to transform into a lycanthrope. Her younger sister desperately attempts to find a cure, but Ginger eventually embraces her newly acquired strength and the sexual appetite it arouses within her. Like The Company of Wolves, Ginger Snaps uses the changing body of the werewolf as a metaphor for the horrors of puberty, menstruation and sexual maturation. Ernest Mathijs (2013) suggests 'the onset of menstruation, the entrance of Ginger into womanhood that signals she is now a sexual being makes her uncontainable and, therefore, monstrous. Put differently, female sexuality provokes horror'.[35] Mathijs further references Briefal's suggestion that 'suffering for female monsters is associated with being sexually active'; in other words, 'if you cease to be a virgin, you cease to be contained, you'll suffer'.[36]

Upon its release, certain critics noted the significant affinity in the subject matter explored by Ginger Snaps and Jordan's film. Linda Ruth Williams wrote 'try to imagine what Buffy the Vampire Slayer would look like if it had been written by Angela Carter and you might get close to the heady cocktail of high-school pubescence and feminist folklore that is Ginger Snaps'.[37] However, the reception and marketing of Fawcett's film is significantly different from that of Jordan's and has perhaps led to The Company of Wolves being overlooked in terms of its relationship with Ginger Snaps. There is a perception of the films as very different, certainly in tone, but also thematically. Indeed, there is only one reference to The Company of Wolves in Mathijs's comprehensive study of Ginger Snaps and this is to note the latter's world premiere in Munich, where several critics drew comparisons between it and Jordan's film. With its scathing humour, bloody effects, contemporary high school setting, teenaged 'outsider' protagonists and self-reflexive irony, Fawcett's film drew comparisons with postmodern horror titles such as *Scream* (1996) and *Buffy the Vampire Slayer* (1997–2003) when it was released in America. While the period setting, literary origins and art-house sensibility of *The Company of Wolves* superficially contrast with the savvy Goth trimmings and Riot Grrrl ethos of *Ginger Snaps*, the core message of both films remains the same. Both titles mount a critique of the oppressive patriarchal construction of women and how this construction conveys the expression of female sexuality as a threat. As Ginger actively embraces her emerging inner beast, *Ginger Snaps* highlights the same deep-rooted cultural attitudes regarding the expression of female desire as *The Company of Wolves*. Like Rosaleen, the Fitzgerald sisters reject taking their pre-allocated places in conventional patriarchal society, a society that, according to Mathijs, 'does not allow girls to refuse to become women-as-defined-by-men'.[38]

FOOTNOTES

1. Email to author
2. Crofts (2003) p126
3. ibid.
4. Email to author
5. Pramaggiore (2008) p33
6. ibid.
7. Crofts (2003) p120
8. Outram (2005) p78
9. Cited in Creed (2002) p67
10. ibid.
11. Zucker (2008) pg61
12. Bourgault du Coudray (2006) p114
13. Bourgault du Coudray (2006) p112
14. Zipes (2012) p22
15. ibid.
16. Reginald & Menville (2005) p90
17. Frost (2003) p81
18. Lovecraft (2008) pg1081
19. Valentine (2008) p52
20. Email to author

21. Email to author
22. Priest (2015) p 3
23. Priest (2015) pp13-14
24. Email to author
25. Evans (1992) p468
26. Creed (1993) 125
27. *The Company of Wolves* (1984): http://www.screenonline.org.uk/film/id/515281/
28. Email to author
29. Stamp (2015) p332
30. Evans (1992) p473
31. Crofts (2003) p119
32. Email to author
33. Email to author
34. Email to author
35. Mathijs (2013) p53
36. Mathijs (2013) p54
37. Williams (2002) p193
38. Mathijs (2013) p58

CHAPTER SEVEN: HAPPILY EVER AFTER...

The Company of Wolves was a pivotal film for many involved in its production. It secured much wider distribution than a lot of other British films at the time and marked the first time a Neil Jordan film would be dubbed into different languages, including French, Spanish, German and Italian. It helped establish Palace Pictures, and Jordan and producer Stephen Woolley have continued to work together throughout their careers. After *The Company of Wolves* Palace Pictures produced several of Jordan's later films, including *Mona Lisa* (1986) and *The Crying Game*, both of which explored themes of identity, gender, infatuation and desire. Prior to its collapse in 1992 it produced several other interesting genre titles including *Dream Demon* (1987), another film concerning female sexual anxiety that unfolds within the Freudian dreamscape of its protagonist, and Richard Stanley's visually striking supernatural horror *Dust Devil* (1992). Jordan and Woolley expressed a strong desire to work with Carter again and prior to her death they discussed the idea of adapting *Vampirella*, another of her radio plays, for cinema. Years later when Woolley sent Jordan the script for *Byzantium* (2013), an adaptation of Moira Buffini's stage play *A Vampire Story* (2008), he described it as 'Angela Carter's *Vampirella*'.[1]

As a ground-breaking British genre film *The Company of Wolves* and its place in horror-fantasy cinema is often overlooked. This may be due to its refusal to be easily categorised. It is a unique beast; part fairy tale, part werewolf film, part horror film, part feminist coming of age allegory. Perhaps it wasn't gory enough for horror fans. Perhaps it proved too potent and grotesque for the art-house crowd. Much has been said of its misjudged US marketing campaign, where the Cannon Group pushed it as a graphic horror movie. Jordan proudly maintains it still stands outside of classification, suggesting it 'doesn't adhere to any shape or type of film',[2] and jokes that perhaps only 'young girls and dogs' can relate to it.[3] He also claimed he wanted it to be rich and adventurous but was wary of being tethered to the limitations of genre. The question of whether it would be commercial never arose in his mind, except at the level of effects, which he maintained had to be satisfying coming in the wake of *An American Werewolf in London* and *The Howling*.

When Jordan presented the finished film to the BBFC he recalled that the absence of any moral lesson in its denouement created confusion and outrage. He surmised that, 'a film with little nudity and less sex was seen as an erotic enticement to teenage girls. […] We had to content ourselves with an 18 certificate, though the film was made with a teenage audience in mind […] it seems that somewhere between the battles against "video nasties" and against the advertising campaign for Pretty Polly tights, a few freedoms are quietly sinking'.[4] Carter recalled that, 'the Thatcherite censorship certainly found it subtly offensive. They couldn't put their finger on it, but they knew that something was wrong'.[5] Stephen Woolley claimed that a few people in the industry warned him that the film would fail because it was too arty for a horror film. Like Rosaleen and the werewolves in the film, Woolley said, 'we kind of had to sit between these two worlds and I think we were conscious of that when we were marketing the film. I think it has a sense of otherworldliness to it, which is, hopefully, timeless […] It's my first movie and I will love it forever whether anyone else likes it or not'.[6]

The film's European marketing campaign didn't overemphasise its horror content; it opted to foreground the film's oddness and dark fantasy elements, and upon its release *The Company of Wolves* met with critical acclaim and moderate commercial success. The European premiere was held at midnight in Leicester Square, London. Wolf handler Tsa Palmer fondly recalls, 'I remember taking the wolves to Leicester Square for the premiere of the film at the Odeon. As I say, wolves are surprisingly adaptable going into these sorts of situations. One of the wolves, Queenie, was quite friendly and happy meeting new people'.[7] With a MPAA 'R' rating, *The Company of Wolves* opened in the US on 19 April, 1985, and made $2,234,776 during its opening weekend, before going on to gross a total of $4,389,334. Distributed by the Cannon Group, it was marketed as a graphic horror film, something Jordan was quite resentful of: 'Cannon [...] did a trailer that made it look like *Friday the 13th*. So it missed its audience in America, but I think it has regained it through the years […] When I was making it I was just trying to reach an area of enchantment that a lot of horror movies seem to miss.'[8] He explained that Cannon's trailer led the audience at the premiere in Times Square to expect blood and guts and that they were confused by what they actually saw: a dark and fantastical exploration of a young girl's sexual awakening.

At the time of its release, *The Company of Wolves* received mixed to positive reviews from critics. Writing for the Chicago Sun-Times Roger Ebert described it as 'a dream about werewolves and little girls and deep, dark forests. It is not a children's film and it is not an exploitation film; it is a disturbing and stylish attempt to collect some of the nightmares that lie beneath the surface of Little Red Riding Hood.' He went on to say that with its 'uncanny, hypnotic force [the film ensures] we always know what is happening, but we rarely know why, or how it connects with anything else, or how we can escape from it, or why it seems to correspond so deeply with our guilts and fears. That is, of course, almost a definition of a nightmare'.[9] Variety commented on the film's combination of grisly effects and fairy tale influences and described it as 'an adult approach to traditional fairy tale material', but noted '[it] nevertheless represents an uneasy marriage between old-fashioned storytelling and contemporary screen explicitness'.[10]

As well as receiving a Special Mention at the 1985 Fantafestival, *The Company of Wolves* also received several Fantasporto awards including the International Fantasy Film Award. Jordan was awarded Director of the Year at the London Critics Circle Film Awards and received several awards from the 1985 Stiges International Film Festival including Prize of the International Critics' Jury. The film was also nominated for the Grand Prize at the Avoriaz Fantastic Film Festival (1985) and various BAFTA Awards (1985) including Best Costume Design (Elizabeth Waller), Best Make Up Artist (Jane Royle, Christopher Tucker), Best Production Design/Art Direction (Anton Furst) and Best Special Visual Effects (Christopher Tucker, Alan Whibley).

A LUPINE LEGACY

With its enduring themes of sexuality and transformation *The Company of Wolves* continues to beguile and intrigue audiences and film-makers. Nicolette Krebitz's *Wild* (2016), a Carter-esque fable of unbound female sexuality, tells of Ania (Lilith Stangenberg), a young woman whose chance encounter with a wolf leads her into an increasingly visceral exploration of primal instincts and bestial sexuality. Becoming fascinated by the wolf, Ania eventually lures it back to her apartment where she isolates herself and, like Rosaleen, begins to not only acknowledge the primal side of her sexuality, but actively explore it. Critic Amber Wilkinson noted it was 'Rooted in the same type of psychosexual myths that inspired Angela Carter's *The Company Of Wolves*,'[11] and *Wild* indeed echoes ideas explored by Carter in *The Bloody Chamber*, particularly 'The Company of Wolves' and 'Wolf-Alice'. As Ania begins to reject the confines of conservative society and free herself of social graces and taboos, Krebitz's screenplay addresses notions of identity, self-actualisation, female sexuality and society's misogynistic construction of gender roles. As Ania embraces her sexual drives and rejects the social conventions that bind her, the film explores and fearlessly depicts exactly how Red Riding Hood came to fall asleep between the paws of a tender wolf and, in the words of Amy Taubin, 'might be the version of Angela Carter's empowering fairy tale […] that Neil Jordan flinched from fully carrying through in his film'.[12]

Several years ago author and producer Brian McGreevy planned to remake *The Company of Wolves*; however Catherine Hardwicke's *Red Riding Hood* had just gone into development at the time, so the idea was shelved. McGreevy cites Jordan's film and Carter's *The Bloody Chamber* as particularly influential on his novel, and its subsequent television adaptation, *Hemlock Grove* (2013–2015). He claimed 'the most immediate influence on *Hemlock Grove* [is] Angela Carter's unsurpassable collection *The Bloody Chamber*'.[13] The author also noted 'to say I was influenced by *The Bloody Chamber* would be an incalculable understatement; it could more accurately be stated that my novel *Hemlock Grove* was one extended piece of Angela Carter fan-fiction […] In a sanitized, digital era when there is increasing dissonance between our NPR brains and our caveman brains with the attendant mass neurosis, Angela's Carter's celebration of the gross excellence of our animal selves is only becoming more relevant'.[14] The transformation sequences in *Hemlock Grove* are especially indebted to Christopher Tucker's work in *The Company of Wolves* and its uncanny depiction of the inner beast emerging from within. McGreevy takes this notion one step further and depicts the human re-emerging from within the beast. This cyclical, ouroboros-esque metamorphosis speaks of continual transformation and rebirth. According to McGreevy it was important to demonstrate 'a ritual death and rebirth, which from the perspective of developmental psychology is this necessary rite of passage between the child self and the adult self'.[15] While some critics claimed *Hemlock Grove* was misogynistic, others suggested that its complex female characters confirmed that 'misogyny isn't the sole domain of men'.[16]

The figure of the wolf-girl and certain ideas Carter explored in 'Wolf-Alice' – such as feral children growing up in the wild and experiencing self-actualisation outside the confines of conservative society – are echoed in Lucky McKee's *The Woman* (2011). While it divided audiences with regards to the authenticity of its self-professed feminist message, *The Woman* violently explores gender relations, the construction of gender roles and depicts various female characters oppressed and brutalised by prevailing patriarchal values. Treading a line between satire and piercing social commentary, *The Woman* is undeniably powerful, but its black and white moralising lacks complexity.

With its exploration of female adolescence, menstruation and rite of passage, *The Company of Wolves* belongs to a specific pack of horror films including *Carrie*, *Ginger Snaps*, *Teeth*, *Jennifer's Body*, *It Follows* and Julia Ducournau's *Raw* (2016). Indeed, Ducournau would explicitly echo Carter's own sentiments when she stated, 'Horror [is] the expression of violence that you feel inside of you – and it's important we recognize that women feel violence and anger as well'.[17] These films use horror to examine themes of female sexuality, identity and transformation. All deal explicitly with the female experience of growing up, the horror of sexuality and adolescent anxiety. The experiences of the young women depicted in these films offer commentary on the restrictive representation of women as constructed by patriarchal society. These titles follow the same path prowled by *The Company of Wolves* in depicting a confrontational femininity, empowering female sexuality and a critique of the ways in which society teaches young women to look at themselves sexually and, more importantly, how to recognise the things they 'should' be afraid of. Like *The Company of Wolves* these films explore the threshold between childhood and adulthood and render it a place where individuals are transformed, literally, figuratively and sometimes monstrously.

The film and the stories upon which it is based have also left their pawprints on the world of music, with bands such as alternative-rock four-piece Wolf Alice and eighties MOR rockers Company of Wolves taking their names from Carter's short stories. Kate Bush was once described as 'covering the territory of Angela Carter's *Company of Wolves* in the guise of a Pre-Raphaelite raised on "Jackie": folkloric fable and disturbed dreams, focusing on the rites of passage between girlishness and womanhood'.[18]

Angela Carter's work has long been a staple in studies of feminism and postmodern literature, and academic interest in *The Company of Wolves* and *The Bloody Chamber* has also become increasingly popular; the latter is now a GCSE set text throughout England and is taught on many university literature courses. In 2015 the University of Hertfordshire hosted a conference on the representation of werewolves, shapeshifters and feral humans in literature, folklore, cinema and popular culture. The conference was named after Jordan's film and was organised by the Open Graves Open Minds research project. It included discussion panels, film screenings, a visit to the UK Wolf Conservation Trust and lectures from fifty keynote speakers and experts in the field, including Sir Christopher Frayling and Neil Jordan. In the words of its co-organiser Kaja Franck, the conference afforded attendees the opportunity to 'learn more about our hirsute alter-egos and what they tell us about being or not-being human'.[19]

The Company of Wolves is many things: a literary adaptation, a coming of age parable, a fantasy film, a horror film, a werewolf film, and a fairy tale. It weaves together myriad connotative references, genres and inspirations to form a rich, full-blooded tapestry that remains as much an enigma today as when it was first released. While it sits as comfortably alongside *Valerie and Her Week of Wonders*, *Pan's Labyrinth* and Catherine Breillat's *Sleeping Beauty* as it does *Ginger Snaps*, *An American Werewolf in London* and *The Howling*, it is also regarded as part of a mid-1980s resurgence in British art cinema alongside titles such as *The Draughtsman's Contract* (1982) and *Caravaggio* (1986), films which 'defiantly turned away from the British realist tradition'.[20] Now over 30 years old, it remains a darkly atmospheric, female-centric coming of age fantasy that is, in the words of Neil Jordan, 'sensual and brutal, like the fairy tale you dreamed of as a child, but were never told'.[21]

FOOTNOTES

1.   Peaty, James (2013) *Interview with Neil Jordan*: http://www.denofgeek.com/movies/neil-jordan/25797/neil-jordan-interview-byzantium-the-company-of-wolves-vampires
2.   *The Company of Wolves* Special Edition DVD Commentary
3.   ibid.
4.   Zucker (2013) pg45
5.   Interview with Angela Carter, https://www.angelacarter.co.uk/interview-for-marxism-todays-left-alive/

6. Producer Stephen Woolley on *The Company of Wolves*: http://www.bfi.org.uk/films-tv-people/4ce2ba0e97bc6

7. Telephone interview with author (10 March, 2016)

8. Edwards (2007) p15

9. Ebert, Roger (1985) http://www.rogerebert.com/reviews/the-company-of-wolves-1985

10. Variety Review (1983) http://variety.com/1983/film/reviews/the-company-of-wolves-1200425940/

11. Wilkinson, Amber (2016) Review of *Wild* http://www.eyeforfilm.co.uk/review/wild-2016-film-review-by-amber-wilkinson

12. Taubin, Amy (2016) Sundance 2016 Preview http://www.filmcomment.com/blog/sundance-2016-preview/

13. Rought, Karen (2014) Interview with Brian McGreevy: http://www.hypable.com/brian-mcgreevy-hemlock-grove-interview/

14. McGreevy, Brian (2014) *The Feminist Horror Author You Need to Read Immediately*: http://www.vulture.com/2014/07/feminist-horror-author-you-need-to-read-now.html

15. Browne, Desiree (2012) *Our Culture Needs Better Monsters* – Interview with Brian McGreevy: https://theawl.com/our-culture-needs-better-monsters-an-interview-with-brian-mcgreevy-b98a6eca3ae1#.hwbe42g50

16. Flint, Mirabelle (2013) *Hemlock Grove and Misogyny*: https://thrillseekingbehaviour.wordpress.com/2013/09/21/hemlock-grove-and-misogyny/

17. Reilly, Phoebe (2016) *From 'The Babadook' to 'Raw': The Rise of the Modern Female Horror Film-maker*: http://www.rollingstone.com/movies/features/the-rise-of-the-modern-female-horror-film-maker-w446369

18. Benson (2001) p50

19. Franck, Kaja (2015) *The Company of Wolves*, 3rd-5th September: http://www.gothic.stir.ac.uk/guestblog/company-of-wolves-conference-3rd-5th-september-2015/

20. Pulver, Andrew (2004) Adaptation of the Week, *The Company of Wolves* (1984): https://www.theguardian.com/books/2004/oct/02/featuresreviews.guardianreview12

21. Zucker (2013) p41

BIBLIOGRAPHY

Anwell, Maggie (1994), 'Lolita Meets the Werewolf: The Company of Wolves', in *The Female Gaze: Women as Viewers of Popular Culture*, ed. Gamman, Lorraine & Marshment, Margaret. London: The Women's Press.

Ashe, Geoffrey (1992), *Mythology of the British Isles*. London: Methuen.

Baring-Gould, Sabine (2014), *Book of Were-Wolves: Were-Wolf History and Folklore*. Milton Keynes: Lightning Source UK.

Beem, Katherine & Paciorek, Andy (2015), *Folk Horror Revival: Field Studies*. Wyrd Harvest Press.

Bell, James (ed.) (2013), *Gothic: The Dark Heart of Film*. London: British Film Institute.

Bell, Mark (1997), 'Production Notes', in *The Curious Room: Collected Dramatic Works*, Carter, Angela. London: Vintage.

Benson, Stephen (2001), 'Angela Carter & the Literary Märchen: A Review', in *Angela Carter and the Fairy Tale*, ed. Bacchilega, Cristina & Roemer, Danielle M. USA: Wayne State University Press.

Bettelheim, Bruno (1976), *The Uses of Enchantment: The Meaning and Importance of Fairy Tales*. New York: Vintage.

Biss, Gerard (2002), *The Door of the Unreal*, Ash Tree Press.

Botting, Fred (2014), *Gothic*. New York: Routledge.

Bourgault du Coudray, Chantal (2006), *The Curse of the Werewolf: Fantasy, Horror and the Beast Within*. London: I.B. Tauris.

Carter, Angela (1995), *The Bloody Chamber*. London: Vintage.

Carter, Angela (1997), *The Curious Room: Collected Dramatic Works*. London: Vintage.

Carter, Angela (2004), *Fireworks*. London: Virago Modern Classics.

Creed, Barbara (1993), 'Dark Desires: Male Masochism in the Horror Film', in *Screening the Male: Exploring Masculinities in Hollywood Cinema*, ed. Cohan, Steven & Hark, Ina Rae. London & New York: Routledge.

Creed, Barbara (2002), 'Horror and the Monstrous-Feminine: An Imaginary Abjection', in *Horror: The Film Reader*, ed. Mark Janovich. London & New York: Routledge.

Crofts, Charlotte (2003), *Anagrams of Desire*. Manchester: Manchester University Press.

De Blécourt, Willem (2015), 'The Case of the Cut-Off Hand: Angela Carter's Werewolves in Historical Perspective', in *She-Wolf: A Cultural History of Female Werewolves*, ed. Priest, Hannah. Manchester Scholarship Online.

Del Toro, Guillermo (2013a), *Cabinet of Curiosities*. London: Titan Books.

Del Toro, Guillermo (2013b), 'Children of the Night', in *Gothic: The Dark Heart of Film*, ed. Bell, James. London: British Film Institute.

Dorson, Richard M. (1982), *Folklore and Folklife: An Introduction*. Chicago: University of Chicago Press.

Duncan, Glen (2013), 'The Werewolf', in *Gothic: The Dark Heart of Film*, ed. Bell, James. London: British Film Institute.

Dundes, Alan (1965), *The Study of Folklore*. New York: Prentice-Hall.

Easton, Alison (2000), 'Introduction: Reading Angela Carter', in *Angela Carter (New Casebooks)*. Hampshire: MacMillan Press.

Edwards, Matthew (2007), 'In the Company of the Wolf: An Interview with Neil Jordan', in *Film Out of Bounds: Essays and Interviews on Non-Mainstream Cinema Worldwide*, ed. Edwards, Matthew. North Carolina: McFarland.

Endore, Guy (1992) *The Werewolf of Paris*, Citadel Press.

Evans, Walter (1992), 'Monster Movies: A Sexual Theory', in *Popular Culture: An Introductory Text*, ed. Lause, Kevin & Nachbar, Jack. Wisconsin: University of Wisconsin Press.

Frayling, Christopher (2015), *Inside The Bloody Chamber: On Angela Carter, the Gothic, and Other Weird Tales*. London: Oberon Books.

Frost, Brian J. (2003), *The Essential Guide to Werewolf Literature*. Wisconsin: The University of Wisconsin Press.

Gamman, Lorraine & Marshment, Margaret (1988), *The Female Gaze*. London: The Women's Press.

Grimm, Jacob & Grimm, Wilhelm (2004), *The Complete Illustrated Works of The Brothers Grimm*. London: Bounty Books.

Gruss, Susanne (2009) *The Pleasure of the Feminist Text: Reading Michèle Roberts and Angela Carter*. Amsterdam & New York: Rodopi.

Hardy, Phil (1999), *Aurum Film Encyclopaedia: Horror*. London: Aurum Press.

Housman, Clemence (2013), *The Were-Wolf*, CreateSpace.

Jones, Darryl (2002), *Horror: A Thematic History in Fiction & Film*. London: Arnold.

Jones, Francis (1992), *The Holy Wells of Wales*. Cardiff: University of Wales Press.

Landis, John (2015), *Monsters in the Movies: 100 Years of Cinematic Nightmares*. London: Dorling Kindersley.

Lopez, Barry (1978), *Of Wolves and Men*. New York: Macmillan Publishing Company.

Lovecraft, H.P. (2008), *Supernatural Horror in Literature, in The Complete Fiction*. New York: Barnes & Noble.

Makinen, Merja (2000), 'Angela Carter's The Bloody Chamber and the Decolonisation of Feminine Sexuality', in *Angela Carter (New Casebooks)*, ed. Easton, Alison. Hampshire: MacMillan Press.

Mathijs, Ernest (2013), *John Fawcett's Ginger Snaps*. Toronto: University of Toronto Press.

Menville, Douglas & Reginald, Robert (2005), *Classics of Fantastic Literature: Selected Review Essays*. Borgo Press.

Munford, Rebecca (2013), *Decadent Daughters and Monstrous Mothers*. Manchester: Manchester University Press.

Newman, Kim (2002), *Science Fiction/Horror: A Sight and Sound Reader*. London: British Film Institute.

O'Donnell, Elliott (1912), *Werwolves*. London. Methuen & Co. [Available at http://www.gutenberg.org]

Orenstein, Catherine (2002), *Little Red Riding Hood Uncloaked: Sex, Morality, and the Evolution of a Fairy Tale*. New York: Basic Books.

Outram, Dorinda (2005), *The Enlightenment*. Cambridge: Cambridge University Press.

Porteous, Alexander (2002), *The Forest in Folklore and Mythology*. New York: Dover.

Pramaggiore, Maria (2008), *Neil Jordan*. Urbana & Chicago: University of Illinois Press.

Priest, Hannah (2015), 'A History of Female Werewolves', in *She-Wolf: A Cultural History of Female Werewolves*. Manchester Scholarship Online.

Reynolds, George W.M. (2006), *Wagner the Werewolf*. Hertfordshire: Wordsworth Editions.

Rigby, Jonathan (2000), *English Gothic: A Century of Horror Cinema*. Surrey: Reynolds & Hearn.

Rockett, Emer & Rockett, Kevin (2003), *Neil Jordan: Exploring Boundaries*. Dublin: Liffey Press.

Sconduto, Leslie A. (2008), *Metamorphoses of the Werewolf: A Literary Study from Antiquity through the Renaissance*. London: McFarland.

Seifert, Lewis C. (2006), *Fairy Tales, Sexuality, and Gender in France, 1690-1715*. Cambridge: Cambridge University Press.

Stamp, Shelley (2015), 'Horror, Femininity, and Carrie's Monstrous Puberty', in *The Dread of Difference: Gender & the Horror Film*, ed. Grant, Barry Keith. Austin: University of Texas Press.

Tatar, Maria (1999), *The Classic Fairy Tales*. New York: W.W. Norton & Company.

Tatar, Maria (2003), *The Hard Facts of the Grimms' Fairy Tales*. Oxfordshire: Princeton University Press.

Valentine, Mark (2008), *The Werewolf Pack*. Hertfordshire: Wordsworth Editions.

Walker, Barbara G. (1983), *The Woman's Encyclopedia of Myths and Secrets*. San Francisco: Harper.

Warner, Marina (1995), *From the Beast to the Blonde: On Fairy Tales and Their Tellers*. London: Vintage.

Williams, Linda Ruth (2002), 'Blood Sisters', in *Science Fiction/Horror: A Sight and Sound Reader*, ed. Newman, Kim. London: British Film Institute.

Wood, Robin (2003), 'The American Nightmare: Horror in the 70s', in *Hollywood: From Vietnam to Reagan… And Beyond*. New York: Columbia University Press.

Zipes, Jack (1993), *The Trials and Tribulations of Little Red Riding Hood*. New York & London: Routledge.

Zipes, Jack (2000a), *Oxford Companion to Fairy Tales*. Oxford: Oxford University Press.

Zipes, Jack (2000b), *The Great Fairy Tale Tradition: From Straparola and Basile to the Brothers Grimm*. New York: W.W. Norton & Company.

Zipes, Jack (2007), *When Dreams Came True: Classical Fairy Tales and Their Tradition*. New York: Routledge.

Zipes, Jack (2012), *Fairy Tales and the Art of Subversion*. Oxon: Routledge Classics.

Zipes, Jack (2013), *The Golden Age of Folk and Fairy Tales: From the Brothers Grimm to Andrew Lang*. Indianapolis: Hackett Publishing Company.

Zipes, Jack (2015), *Grimm Legacies: The Magic Spell of the Grimms' Folk and Fairy Tales*. New Jersey: Princeton University Press.

Zucker, Carole (2008), *Dark Carnival: The Cinema of Neil Jordan*. London: Wallflower Press.

Zucker, Carole (2013), *Neil Jordan: Interviews*. Jackson: University Press of Mississippi.